THE JOURNEY TO SUCCESS

A BLUEPRINT FOR WINNING IN BUSINESS & LIFE

GARY HARTFIELD

PUBLISHING

CONTENTS

Paperback ISBN: 979-8-9912197-0-9

For My Family

INTRODUCTION

Chances are, you picked up this book because, for some reason, success, however you define it, has eluded you. I want to assure you that I believe you will substantially increase your chances by internalizing and applying this book's teachings.

Life has its many trials and tribulations, as we all know, but it also has many pleasantries and blessings. One of the major blessings of my life, something I absolutely love doing, is helping, teaching, and mentoring entrepreneurs, aspiring leaders and business owners. I found that giving away the knowledge I've accrued through experience, mentors, and books serves twofold. Selflessly, it serves the person I am helping, but also, selfishly, it serves me in being able to master the information better.

Legacy isn't often discussed in your twenties, thirties, or forties, but leaving the right one has always been important to me. By writing this book, or better said, by YOU reading this book, I humbly hope that it helps you and, whether we know each other or not, you reach the destination of success you're looking for and you help someone else, thus becoming a part of my legacy and adding onto it.

I founded Empower Florida, Inc. in 2015 because I knew there were tens of thousands of business owners (including their staff) in Florida who, like me at one time, were hurting for the proper education, timely information, and empowerment in persons living with disabilities. I knew that if agency owners were better informed, they would be empowered to develop and maintain viable businesses that create employment opportunities and provide high-quality services for the wonderful people who we love and provide services for.

By helping and training the owners to grow their mindsets, we've helped them understand the accountability of their ministry as well as areas of accounting, insurance, banking, legal representation, and other areas that "mom and pop" owners don't pay enough attention to. I'm so proud to say we've helped more than 20,000 people! I hope also to help you.

Success, like confidence, is not a place that you arrive at and can remain there infinitely. Success is like a muscle. It must be exercised and properly cared for to sustain it. Once you reach your goal, you set other goals. Getting my bachelor's degree was great, but then I went on to earn my Master's in Business Administration. I reached my goal of owning an assisted living facility but then I wanted another one, and another one. I've owned and operated several facilities that provide care for the elderly and developmentally disabled. Then, I got into insurance and opened my insurance company in 2012.

If I had to identify my entrepreneurial profile, it would be a "builder." I am motivated by and passionate about building people and businesses.

I wrote this book so that at one point, you think back of the seventeen-year-old you and humbly and gratefully know in your heart that your young self would be proud of who you've become. What brings me joy when I think of the seventeen-year-old me is that I haven't lived my life trying to just accumulate money and wealth; I've also gone out of my way many times to help others.

My name is Gary, which means, Mighty with a Spear, Spear Carrier, and Strong Man of God. I've been named a warrior since the day of my birth. Because we don't live in medieval times, my battles are not on battlegrounds or in arenas, but in helping individuals, families, and communities. Please allow my thoughts and words to come alongside you as you fight for the life you were destined and equipped to live.

I hope this book falls into the hands of a young person dreaming about a higher level of education, maybe even a post-secondary education. I hope it falls in the hands of a man recently released from prison who feels the world is against him and that he can never be successful. I hope it falls in the hands of a single mother who just can't seem to catch a break with her finances; regardless of how hard she works. I hope it falls into a young couple's hands as they plan for a great future, so they learn lessons here that they don't have to painfully experience. I hope it falls into the hands of the broken-hearted, spiritually-wounded, divorced person, and someone who just needs a little more air underneath their wings.

Ultimately, I wrote this book for you because you're the one holding it. Amidst this crazy world, somehow, some way, this book has fallen into your hands. I believe that it's your time to realize your Magnum Opus—Great Work. You didn't come by this book through chance or happenstance; I believe it was ordained for this time of your life to learn these infallible rules of success because you are the chosen one in your family to break the cycle of failure and poverty.

CHAPTER 1
TRIALS AND TRIBULATIONS

NO ONE IS PERFECT

Most of us would like to live perfect lives—no stress, no drama, marry the ideal spouse, raise perfect kids, make money while we sleep, be able to travel wherever, whenever, have loving and dependable friends, and leave an amazing legacy. Not one person that I know wakes up hoping to go through trials or tribulations. However, the perfect world doesn't exist here on earth.

The undeniable truth is that every person goes through trials and tribulations. Jesus himself stated, "In this world, you will have tribulation," and He hasn't been wrong yet. Sure, trials and tribulations are challenging, sometimes frustrating enough to bring you to tears, but you must understand that the road to success goes through trials and tribulations.

Your journey to success is no different than the other 8 billion people on the planet. Those who embrace it, knowing that something good will come from it, live happier lives than those who cry and complain about it. Which one do you want to be?

The great Nelson Mandela, a symbol of resilience and triumph over adversity, provides profound wisdom that perfectly describes the truth of soul-strengthening power through trials:

 Difficulties break some men but make others. No axe is sharp enough to cut the soul of a sinner who keeps on trying, one armed with the hope that he will rise even in the end.

NELSON MANDELA

Mandela's quote is founded on the idea that handling adversity the right way has the power to either break us or make us stronger. Many modern-day "gurus" today talk in hypotheticals, having never journeyed the paths they tell their followers to walk. When it comes to the subject of trials, Mandela has walked it. His long struggle against apartheid and imprisonment for 27 years were monumental trials. However, he emerged as a powerful leader and a beacon of hope and strength.

There are quite a few takeaways I hope become embedded into your mind and spirit from this book. However, if there can be only one, it's this—the road to success is fraught with trials. However, it is how you go through the tests that will determine how successful you will become.

The answer now, dear reader, is, what is success to you?

WHAT IS SUCCESS?

One of the most common metrics for success is the accumulation of wealth and material possessions. Society often equates financial abundance with a successful life. My issue with this limited view is that it leaves out the numerous other facets of human well-being. For example, if you are wealthy but lose your family because of the amount of time you invest in your career, are you successful? If you are wealthy but work yourself to the point that you get a potentially life-threatening illness, are you successful? If you are wealthy but have lied and cheated your way there and now no one likes or respects you, are you successful?

True success is a concept far more profound and diverse than what is often depicted in popular culture or reality shows. It goes beyond mere material wealth, fame, and professional accomplishment, although those are certainly by-products. True success must also encompass well-being, meaningful relation-ships, personal growth, positive contributions to society, resilience, and emotional intelligence. That is why, to be truly successful, one of the fundamental requirements is having good character, described as the mental and moral qualities distinctive to an individual.

Character cannot be developed in ease and quiet.

Only through experience of trial and suffering

can the soul be strengthened, ambition inspired,

and success achieved.

HELEN KELLER

The most inspiring part of this quote to me is none other than the woman who wrote it. Considering her incredibly challenging life and seeing the spirit of will win out, is nothing short of remark-able. Her credibility gives her words validity.

In today's digital age, popularity on social media has become a conventional way of defining success for many individuals. While I concede that the number of followers, likes, shares, and comments offer instant gratification, it's essential to understand that the online world is often a superficial representation of one's life. In other words, social media can make people feel like "The

Man" or "The Boss Babe," but when they turn off the app, they're still paying rent in the same apartment, driving the same old car, and striving to make ends meet. Although mirages are most common in dry deserts, they're becoming a staple of many online personas.

One of the issues of social media popularity equating to success is that, aside from providing content, there is no real struggle. Beware of when things come too easily, when they're not worked for.

It could sway you to believe that everything will be this way, that you are lucky, that the undeniable secrets to success don't have anything to do with you. Don't fall for the lie that life will always be easy. When things come too quickly, a sense of entitlement grows within a person's subconscious.

"BEWARE OF WHEN THINGS COME TOO EASILY, WHEN THEY'RE NOT WORKED FOR."

CONSIDER YOURSELF BLESSED

For those who live in the United States of America, consider yourself fortunate. Although our history and present-day have legitimate warts, it's still the best country, in my opinion. The success of the United States of America has made it easy for its citizens to prosper, which has allowed for a sense of entitlement to grow like unchecked weeds. Just because you have the same degree as your predecessor who was promoted in two years doesn't mean you're going to get promoted in two years just because you come in on time every day. Progress must always be worked for.

Like us adults, our kids here can go to school free of charge, and with so much information and freedom in this country, they can become whatever they work for. The number one thing that holds them back is that they feel it will materialize with minimum effort. Wake up. It won't.

I'm tired of seeing people of all walks of life complain about their job, complain that they only get two weeks of vacation a year and don't earn enough to go anywhere, complain about this, complain about that—but never change their daily habits! Five years, ten years, and even fifty years later, they're complaining about the same things as they unsuccessfully try to get comfortable on their deathbeds! There is a way out of poverty and mediocrity and I'd love to show it to you.

God built me to be an educator at heart. Sharing is a natural extension of who I am. Very few things in life give me more pleasure than imparting wisdom to someone and seeing it motivate the person to take action and see that action manifest something of value for the individual. I believe it is one of the reasons why I'm here.

In 2013, my dear friend Valerie Goddard handed me a fascinating book. The title was, The Journey to Success, and it had a lovely cover. I anxiously opened the book to find something valuable I could include in my daily life. However, every page was blank! I looked up at her for answers.

Then she said, "It's up to you to fill the pages of this book. Take the life lessons you've gained in your success journey and share them in a way that would be meaningful to others.

Today, you hold the book I held in 2013, except that the pages have been filled with what, I pray, will help mold and shape you and your mindset so that you can find the purpose God has destined for you.

THIS BOOK

Contained in this book are answers you have been searching for, even if you didn't know the questions. I have poured factual accounts, anecdotes, real stories of others, and some of my life, even the painful and embarrassing ones onto these pages.

Sure, you're going to go through trials.

Sure, you're going to go through tribulations.

Sure, sometimes you'll feel like you're going in the opposite direction of success.

Sure, you'll question whether you're smart, strong, equipped, or supported enough to materialize your dreams.

Sure, it is not going to be easy. In fact, it might be a dogfight of epic proportions.

Sure, there will be times when you'll stare face to face with fear in the darkness of the night.

However, there are certainties on the other side of fear as well.

Should you empower yourself with the right mindset and consistently take the right actions:

Surely, you'll find out you're not on an island.

Surely, the right help will come at the right time.

Surely, there is a solution to every problem.

Surely, God has not punished you.

Surely, the trials you've gone through have strengthened and equipped you.

Surely, God has plans for you, and they are good.

Surely, whatever God brings you to, believe, and he will get you through.

As proof of what I've written in this first chapter, for many of you, bad or unfortunate events will come up that will make it challenging to finish this book.

> "I BELIEVE YOU ARE HOLDING THIS BOOK, WHENEVER THIS BOOK FINDS YOU, FOR THIS SEASON YOU ARE IN RIGHT NOW."

I believe you are holding this book, whenever this book finds you, for this season you are in right now. I don't believe in coincidences, which means there's a purpose for you to be this close to the wisdom and lessons contained herein at this particular juncture in life.

I urge you to give the future, better you, every chance of becoming the present you. Grab a highlighter and a notebook, and allow me to guide you through *The Journey to Success*.

CHAPTER 2
RESILIENCY

I love the embodiment of the word—resiliency. The word is defined in two different (but similar) ways:

1. The capacity to recover quickly from difficulties; toughness.
2. The ability of a substance or object to spring back into its original shape; elasticity.

Every person on this planet has embodied the word resiliency in his or her lifetime. Meaning you, dear reader, have as well. If you're reading this book, there is a drive in you, a resiliency that wants to fight back against the cards life has dealt you, and you are determined to leave this planet better than how you entered it through your success.

However, the word resiliency is only used if a setback provokes it. You only need to be resilient if you get tested. You'll never reap the courage from knowing you are resilient if something terrible never happens. So, while I love the word, I cringe at the provocation of it.

4 DAYS FROM CHRISTMAS

I had gone through my tests and trials. Yet, one hurt me unlike any other. My sister, Tammy Laconya Hartfield, and I were unable to execute our initial plan of purchasing what we thought was our dream assisted living facility. While I was busy spitting out the bitter taste of defeat, Tammy came up with the brilliant idea of buying a smaller existing facility near St. Petersburg, Florida.

After some research, many internal conversations, and some interaction with their management, we visited a small, eight-bed facility in Seminole, FL. After negotiating with the owner, Tammy and I finalized the deal. The purchase agreement was $170,000 for the facility and $30,000 for the business, totaling $200,000.

We were ecstatic! We went to Macaroni Grill for a celebratory lunch, where we thanked God and talked excitedly about the many next steps required to manifest our dreams. We were officially on our way to becoming successful. The task ahead of us was monumental, but we had already killed the giant; now, all we had to do was cut its head off, and we were equipped with swords.

After an exhilarating but exhausting lunch, Tammy went to work as a waitress at a local restaurant. "I like my job there, but I can't wait to give my resignation. Feel me, Big Bro?"

"I can't wait either. Now get to work before you show up late and you don't have a job to quit!" I lay down and took a nap; when I awoke, I drove to Sanford and picked up my daughter Ashley.

At around 7 AM the following day, I was awakened by a disturbing phone call from my father explaining that the paramedics could not get Tammy to breathe. In the fog of being woken up, I couldn't wrap my mind around the meaning of his words—*can't get Tammy to breathe.*

Given Tammy's past experiences, I thought she was sick or hurt but, like always, she would be fine. Life had tried to beat her up, but she had elasticity; she always bounced back with the same smile and friendly nature. Besides, Baby Sis and I had some serious plans, and nothing was going to get in the way. I hung up the phone, lay back down, and dismissed a nagging thought that I should be worried.

My father called back several minutes later. "She's dead, Gary."

My heart jumped into my throat and an intense pressure squeezed my brain. "Wait. Dad. Hold on. What's going on?"

"Gary," he sobbed. "She's gone. Tammy's gone."

Approximately 14 hours after we had closed a life-changing deal, my baby sister was dead. I got off my bed to pace, to run, to punch something, to pray, to call someone, anyone, but instead, I fell to my knees, weak and profoundly sad. I had never known the definition of sorrow until that moment.

"My baby's dead!" I yelled repeatedly. I had never experienced such a profound emotional loss. I didn't know how to handle it. I let out a primal scream, maybe in that scream I tried to emote what I couldn't verbally express. Tammy had taken an overdose of OxyContin and died from respiratory arrest.

Ashley burst into my room to see what was happening. She found her proud, tall, strong father, which many people respected, look beaten and broken. It was the first time she had seen me cry.

"Dad…" It was as if she didn't know what to say.

"Tammy… Oh God Ashley, Tammy's gone!" I sobbed unashamedly.

Ashley ran to me and hugged me tightly from behind while tears started to form in her eyes. I felt her start to heave, as she too started to cry.

"Oxycontin," I mumbled.

"No, no, no, dad this can't be happening!'

For a brief moment I thought to hug Ashley and comfort her. However, my grief was too strong. We stayed there for a while. While it was the saddest part of my life, in a way, it was an incredible bonding moment with my daughter.

As if losing a cherished, loved sibling that I had plans with wasn't bad enough, we closed on the business on December 21, 2002. We were just days away from celebrating Christmas, the perfect time to share our momentous occasion with the family. Instead of preparing for Christmas and celebrating like a family, we had to plan my youngest sister's funeral services.

Personally, I was a wreck. It was so unfair. Do I get mad at her and live with that for the rest of my life? I had no answers. Professionally, I didn't know what to do. Tammy was going to leave her job to be the boots on the ground at the new facility we purchased. *Do I sell the contract? Will I go through this pain every time I enter the facility?*

I will tell you unashamedly that I went through a period of tears, anger, and confusion. Yet, God let me know something powerful.

We are built for storms. Boats aren't built to be tied to the dock; they're created to go over rough waters and still reach their destination.

"WE ARE BUILT FOR STORMS."

Indeed, trials and tribulations test our mettle, push us beyond our comfort zones, and force us to confront our limitations. When faced with adversity, if we can summon up the courage, we can dig deep into our reserves of strength, resilience, and determination. The process of confronting difficulties and overcoming them is a crucible that forges a stronger, more resilient soul.

I chose to press forward with the plans Tammy and I conceived. Twenty-plus years later, and the results have been amazing. I have tried to honor your dream, baby sis. I love you."

CRUSHING

I'm certainly not the only one who has gone through adversity. As I wrote in the first chapter, adversity is a prerequisite to success. Bishop T.D. Jakes said it best in a sermon:

I have never met anybody who became incredibly successful

in any area of their life until they have

suffered and sweated and sacrificed

and kept their focus and fought through tears

and trials and tests.

If you have a dream and you commit to it,

it will come to pass.

T.D. JAKES

If you know of T.D. Jakes, you may think, doesn't he have one of the most successful ministries in the world? Besides preaching, isn't he also a New York Times best-selling author? Besides preaching and writing, doesn't he also produce hit movies? What would such a successful and beloved pastor know about real adversity—the type real people go through?

In the first chapter of Jake's book, *Crushing*, he shares a crushing moment in his life as his then thirteen-year-old daughter, Sarah, informs him and his wife that she is pregnant. In this bitter-sweet moment, as tears flowed from his eyes, he was also reminded of the recent death of one of his closest confidants who had been the bedrock of his life, his mother, who would not be a great-grandmother to the unexpected child to come.

Simultaneously, his ministry was being blessed abundantly. His books were bestsellers, he was being asked to speak at venues worldwide, and movie producers were interested in taking his book, "Woman, Thou Art Loosed!" to the big screen.

However, he still had to grapple with the inevitable PR crisis that would call into question his ministry by way of his effectiveness as a father. He braced himself for the inevitable question: How can you lead churches and minister to others all over the world when you can't even protect your thirteen-year-old daughter from getting pregnant while so young and living in your home?

Bishop Jakes went on to write, "Such was my season at that time. I felt trapped in my pain. Leveled by circumstances beyond my control. Powerless to protect those I loved the most. Unable to enjoy my life's many blessings. Crushed."

If you follow Bishop Jakes, you know that his ministry has grown since then. Indeed, he showed resilience in a situation that would have forced others to draw away from the limelight and "circle the wagons" around the family until the fervor died down. At the time of this writing, Sarah has proven to walk in her father's footsteps. She is an author, entrepreneur, media personality, and a pastor at One Church alongside her husband.

Adversity comes in a myriad of ways. The one I shared about Tammy centered on a death while the one I shared about Jakes centered on a life. You will advertently or inadvertently create your fair share of troubles, but also, those in our circle, even the ones you love the most, can bring adversity and chaos to you, as was the case with the stories I shared.

At the end of the day, it doesn't matter where adversity comes from. What matters is if you have the toughness and elasticity to confront it, overcome it, and learn from it so you design a life that mitigates the same ones from happening. You may consider finally not hanging around the people who continue to bring drama and trauma to your life. Consider looking up some videos on YouTube for the side hustle you want to start instead of watching the game or binge-watching catty shows that don't edify your mind or spirit.

Be sure to pack enough resiliency on your journey to success. It doesn't matter if you feel you've had a lifetime of bad times; more will come. Those who tend to fall prey to continual bad times are those who never learn from them. Resilience is not merely the ability to bounce back from failure; it is also having the strength to endure and persist through challenging circumstances.

In the upcoming chapters, I will share tangible dos and don'ts for success. But first, let's find your Unique Purpose!

CHAPTER 3
UNCOVERING YOUR UNIQUE PURPOSE

 "The purpose of life is not to be happy. It is to be useful, to be honorable, to be compassionate, to have it make some difference that you have lived and lived well."

RALPH WALDO EMERSON

WHAT IS PURPOSE?

A life without purpose is meaningless. It's like eating tasteless food that brings no nourishment to your body. You go through the motions, but there's no enjoyment of the process, and it doesn't yield results. What is life worth without finding its purpose?

More than 8 billion people are walking the face of this earth, more than any other time in human history. What do you think is the percentage of people alive today walking in their purpose? You have to take into account the many countries whose citizens aren't allowed to reach further than their parents did or have been placed in a class they can never break free from. Likewise, there are those who don't have the means or technologies to leave the rice fields, mountainsides, hillsides, or farms where they struggle daily to survive.

Then, consider the people in the United States who are shamed for going against societal expectations and embracing their true selves. While there are no statistics to prove how many people today live without true purpose, my guess is that at least 5 billion people live without hope, without true joy, and without purpose. There is a good chance that you are among them, dear reader. My assignment in this chapter is to educate you on what purpose is and guide you in finding it.

Our inner purpose is the compass that directs us toward a life of fulfillment and meaning. Unlike external markers of success, inner purpose is not a destination; it's an ongoing journey, a continuous, honest exploration of one's self that provides clarity and direction. Your inner purpose is discovering your "aliveness" and eventually unearthing the talents innately given to you that make you most alive as you gift them to the world.

Grab some scuba gear and let's get into deeper waters…

YOUR INNER SELF

Before discovering your purpose, you need to know your inner self. Who you are currently is the subconscious repository of your thoughts, memories, experiences, emotions, and other aspects of your mind.

In simpler terms, you are who you think you are or should be. Chances are, you're reading this book because you don't like where you are in life, or you feel like you should be further along, whether financially, physically, relationship-wise, or emotionally. I submit

"IN SIMPLER TERMS, YOU ARE WHO YOU THINK YOU ARE OR SHOULD BE."

to you to grab a pen and paper and believe there is a reason—a purpose—that you hold this book in your hands at this particular juncture in your life. You are meant to do this exercise at a time such as this.

Mark Twain famously wrote, *"The two most important days in your life are the day you are born and the day you find out why."* How about we make today one of the most important days of your life and find out why you were born? Come on. You can do it! Be courageous. You're worth it.

TWELVE ACTIONS TO UNCOVER YOUR INNER PURPOSE

Reflect on Passions and Interests:

Start your journey by reflecting on the activities and interests that genuinely ignite your enthusiasm for life. Consider what brings you joy and fulfillment in your personal, social, and professional life. Identifying your passions is foundational in uncovering the elements that could contribute to your unique purpose. Your creator would not instill in you your particular passions without a reason. What are they? Write them down.

A way to distinguish things you like and are passionate about is with this analogy: A joke can make you laugh (things you like) but an upcoming event can make you sing and smile all day (things you're passionate about).

Assess Your Strengths and Skills:

Take a thorough inventory of your strengths and skills. What are the things you excel at naturally? What comes easier to you than to others? Is it your unique way of cooking; or your ability to understand gears, motors, and gadgets; or your uncanny way of understanding technology without being taught; or your natural ability to connect with people verbally; or your green thumb that grows any flower or garden or your talent to produce or play music; or the ability to assess good business deals with little information?

Recognizing your unique talents provides insight into how you can leverage your abilities to make a meaningful impact on your life and others. Your strengths often align closely with your purpose, forming a solid foundation for a purpose-driven life.

Define Your Core Values:

Your core values are the guiding principles that shape your decisions and actions. Reflect on the values that matter most to you. What principles do you hold dear, and what virtues do you prioritize? Aligning your purpose with your core values ensures that your life's journey is in harmony with your deeply held beliefs, fostering authenticity and fulfillment.

What are your core values? What things would you never do regardless of any money or fame offered you? Your values might be aligned with a fantastic non-profit you are designed to help or things going on today that you are intended to oppose. You'll never know if you don't define your core values.

If you are still simply reading this without writing your unique answers down, ask yourself why. Be mindful that the current you is at war with the future, better you. You will tell yourself you don't need this exercise but challenge that rationale. Go back to the beginning of the twelve actions and write down answers that have the power to uplift and free you.

Explore the Intersection of Passion and Contribution:

Delve into the space where your passions intersect with the potential to positively contribute to the world. Consider how your unique combination of interests, skills, and values can address needs or create positive change in your community or beyond. This intersection often holds the key to discovering a purpose that is both personally meaningful and impactful.

Understand this—your purpose is not to get rich, although that can certainly be a by-product; your objective is to ultimately help your fellow man. In the Bible, we find that young David was an amazing harp player. However, David's purpose in playing the harp was not to sell out venues; it was for the demons to flee from King Saul, giving him the ability to think rationally and behave righteously.

> **"WE'LL NEVER KNOW HOW MANY PEOPLE DAVID SAVED BY PLAYING THE HARP FOR THE TORMENTED KING."**

We'll never know how many people David saved by playing the harp for the tormented king. How can your passions, strengths, skills, and core values help your community?

Embrace Continuous Learning and Adaptability:

The journey to finding your unique purpose is dynamic and evolving. Embrace a mindset of continuous learning and adaptability. Be open to new experiences, challenges, and insights. Sometimes, your purpose may reveal itself through unexpected avenues. Cultivate a willingness to grow, evolve, and refine your understanding of your unique purpose over time.

At one time, my purpose was to get into the assisted living facility industry. Today, through learning many lessons, taking chances, and being coachable, my purpose is more about educating people, particularly minorities with limiting mindsets and generational curses, on how to break free from the yoke of financial, illiterate, spiritual, relational, and emotional slavery. You, too, are meant to evolve, so be on the lookout for new opportunities, paths, mentors, and topics.

Engage in Mindfulness Practices:

Incorporate mindfulness practices into your routine, such as meditation or reflective journaling. These activities can help you connect with your inner self, quiet the noise of external influences, and clarify your desires and aspirations. Mindfulness creates a space for introspection, making identifying the elements that contribute to your unique purpose easier.

Imagine journaling for 12 months and then looking back at the things that used to bring you anxiety and how everything played out. This could help you silence depression and anxiety. You'll also identify things you've been worried about or complaining about for the entire 12 months and finally bring you to the point of solving the issue once and for all. How would you be able to free yourself from these types of fears and limiting beliefs if you don't journal? Can you envision yourself 12 months from now after doing this exercise just 10-15 minutes a day? How much stronger would your resolve be? Don't you think that could change your life?

Seek Diverse Experiences:

Expand your horizons by seeking out diverse experiences. Exposure to different cultures, environments, and perspectives can broaden your understanding of the world and expose you to new passions or causes. These varied experiences may hold the key to uncovering aspects of yourself that contribute to your unique purpose.

Go to places you would typically not go—so long as it doesn't go against your core values. Find someone to have a sensible dialogue about your differences, whether they are spiritual or political. Speak to enlighten and listen to understand. You may find out this world is not as divided as the media would have you believe, which, by itself, would enrich your quality of life and make you more joyful and less resentful. Write down new places you will go. Write down the titles of people you need to meet to further your career and get you closer to your goals.

Connect with Mentors and Role Models:

Seek guidance from mentors and role models who inspire you. Engaging with individuals who have walked a similar path or have insights to share can provide valuable perspectives on purpose and personal growth. Their experiences can serve as inspiration and guidance as you navigate your journey to find your unique purpose.

Someone has likely been or is where you'd like to be. Stop asking your single girlfriends or divorced "homies" for marital advice. Stop taking financial advice from your uncle, who struggles to keep an apartment and can't afford his own car. I firmly believe in respecting my elders, but if I had taken advice from all of them, I would have never reached the level of success I have and would not be in a position to impart experienced knowledge to you in this, my second book. Choose wisely who you allow to water the garden of your thoughts.

Finding the right mentors and applying their knowledge will hasten your ability to find your true purpose and shorten the road to success.

Write down a Champions List—a list of people you respect that you will reach out to. Invite some of them to coffee or lunch and ask them to mentor you by phone or lunch once a month or a quarter.

Volunteer and Give Back:

Engage in volunteer activities or contribute to causes that resonate with you. Acts of service and giving back to the community make a positive impact and provide a sense of purpose. By aligning your actions with your values, you may discover a deeper connection to a cause or mission that reflects your unique purpose.

Giving back is a proven philosophy for growth and wealth. Sure, today, many wealthy people give to charities and such for tax benefits or for pats on the back but giving 10% of one's earnings to God has been around since the earliest days of man. If you can find a way to bless others, either with money or volunteering your time or knowledge, God will find a way to bless you! If you aren't sure where to start and are a believer, start with your church.

Conduct Purposeful Networking:

Connect with individuals who share similar interests or are passionate about causes you find meaningful. Attend events, join online communities, or participate in workshops related to your areas of interest. Meaningful connections can provide insights, support, and collaborative opportunities that contribute to the unfolding of your unique purpose.

There's a saying that has stood the test of time because of its validity—it's not what you know; it's who you know!

Embrace Vulnerability:

Embrace vulnerability as a pathway to authenticity. Acknowledge your fears and insecurities, for it is in vulnerability that you uncover your true self and, consequently, your inner purpose.

Superman and Wonder Woman only exist in the DC Universe. It's okay not to have all the answers. How can anyone help you if they think you always have everything under control? I'm not suggesting you put all your fears and personal business on social media, but be open with yourself and those God has placed in your path.

Seek Feedback:

Engage with trusted friends, mentors, or colleagues to gain insights into your strengths and areas for growth. External perspectives can provide valuable perspectives on your inner purpose.

Too many people can't decipher between constructive criticism and criticism. Take your ego out of the equation. The person giving you feedback focuses on the issue or an isolated situation, not on you. Even if you disagree, don't argue or you may risk the person never bothering to try to help you again. Seeking feedback is closely tied to embracing vulnerability. Through this "weakness," you can become incredibly strong.

MANIFEST DESTINY

As you embark on the journey to uncover your inner purpose, remember that it is a dynamic process of self-discovery and growth, so this should be fun and exciting! Embrace the uniqueness of your path, for within it lies the key to unlocking your best life.

Your inner purpose is not a destination but a continuous journey, an ever-unfolding story that shapes the narrative of your existence. May this chapter be a guide, illuminating the path to a life rich with purpose, joy, and fulfillment.

If you wrote down everything I asked, you have a collection of words, names, places, and actions that will help you find your purpose and manifest it! If you haven't written anything down, you can do so now, the next chapter will wait patiently for you.

CHAPTER 4
VISION, PROCESS, AND NOISE

THE VISION

Everyone wants the benefits, accolades, awards, financial freedom, a great marriage, wonderful and respectful children, an amazing career, and everything they consider what success is in life—but few want to go through the process of obtaining it. If living your dreams were easy, you'd already be there.

The truth is—while achieving your goals is one of the most rewarding feelings in life, it's also one of the most difficult. I've heard it said, "God will give the vision to get to the next level, whether it's growing the business, growing the church, or developing the ministry, but he won't share with you the process. If He did, most would shun it."

Whether you consider yourself spiritual or not, whatever vision you have for your life, as clear as it may be, the process of discovering it is hidden. You may feel like you know how to get from A to B and then end up at C, but the road to success has many hidden curves, pitfalls, ambushes, and desert-like mirages; you may think you've made it to your destination only to find it's all smoke and mirrors and there's still a long way to go.

In business, it starts with a comprehensive business plan. If you're not willing and patient enough to set aside the time, make the sacrifices, and do the research to write a comprehensive business plan, you won't likely have the wherewithal required to succeed. It's best not to start the business if you can't discipline yourself to create a compelling and sensible business plan.

Your version of alignment will be unique to you—and, make no mistake, it will require you to be fully present, engaged, committed, and open to evolution. Maybe, like me, you'll need to reexamine how, when, where, and with whom you are working within your current business model.
Michelle Jacobik
The Path To Profits:
An Entrepreneurs Guide To Having It All... And Still Having A Life!

I have heard many close friends, colleagues, peers, and associates discuss ideas I thought were fabulous, yet, sadly, most of them never acted on them. Dr. Miles Monroe once said that the grave is the wealthiest place on earth because brilliant, million-dollar ideas have been buried with those who had them but lacked the courage to make them come true.

I'll ask you, dear reader, what ideas have you let slip through your now empty hands?

Are you like many others who thought of something and never acted on it, only to see a version of it in a television commercial and say, "Hey, I thought of that!"

I will ask you a couple of questions, but before I do, don't worry about HOW it will happen. Tony

STEPHEN PRESSFIELD ONCE STATED, "MOST OF US HAVE TWO LIVES--THE LIFE WE LIVED AND THE UNLIVED LIFE WITHIN US."

Robbins, the world's foremost "Self-Help Guru," warns people about—The Tyranny of How. A tyranny is an oppressive government that doesn't allow its citizens to do what they like or can. I want you to eliminate the HOW you will do it and focus solely on what your heart desires.

I urge you to actively and interactively go through this book; don't just passively read it; you'll rob yourself of the power in these pages.

Ready? Here are my two questions—do yourself a favor and write them down and answer them:

What vision do you have for yourself?

Where do you see yourself in five years?

Whatever your answers are, you can get it if you believe it, but there is a process.

There will be challenges. There will be betrayals. There will be haters. There will be partners who knowingly defraud you or, like my baby sister, leave you much too soon. Here's the crazy thing—if it doesn't get tough, you're not on the right path.

> **"THERE WILL BE CHALLENGES. THERE WILL BE BETRAYALS. THERE WILL BE HATERS."**

THE PROCESS

For me, the process was to identify a mentor, conduct massive research, have patience, and then take action even if everything wasn't perfectly laid out. I didn't just jump into owning an assisted living facility; that would have been disastrous for my career, my employees, and most importantly, to those exceptional individuals who deserve to live out the rest of their days with the proper care, dignity, and respect.

Identifying a mentor sometimes isn't enough. First, you need to find the right mentor. Then, you have to get that mentor to buy in to what your plans are. In order to do that, you have to be open, vulnerable, and willing not just to learn but apply the knowledge handed down to you. After all, knowledge is not power; applied knowledge is power.

This individual believed in me and allowed me to shadow him for more than a year. Watching someone walk in the shoes you want to buy is much different than admiring the shoes online or at a shoe store. I also did plenty of research by visiting other facilities. I was always respectful but inquisitive. It was imperative for me to know their process for success. I was keenly interested in how and in what avenues they marketed their facility and whom they targeted. I was also focused on how they promoted themselves. I needed to know how they fostered a community that would align with their targeted community.

I left no stone unturned; I even found out where they placed their beds and how they made the rooms inviting for a resident or a son or daughter looking at it for the first time to decide if it was good enough for their elderly parent. I had plenty of theoretical knowledge, but with lives at stake, that wasn't enough, so I got real-world, practical knowledge that I could emulate or surpass.

As you may have guessed by how I started this chapter, I wrote a comprehensive business plan before starting. Included in my business plan was a detailed strategy for every functional part of the business! I wrote one for marketing, finance, operations, food and beverage, hospitality, trash disposal—everything! I realized I had to immerse myself to reach the milestone I longed for. Once I was in business and my team and I had more real-world experiences under our belt, the business plan evolved. Remember that your business plan is a living, breathing, and growing document. It should evolve as your business evolves.

"I DIDN'T HAVE A SILVER BULLET OR A MAGIC WAND – I HAD A WORK ETHIC AND TENACITY."

I'm humbled but also proud to say that I was able to sell a significant portion of the business in 2019. I had reached that goal. Mind you, dear reader, that I didn't have a silver bullet or a magic wand—I had a work ethic and tenacity, but most of all, I went after my dreams.

Before success comes in any man's life, he is sure to meet with much temporary defeat, and, perhaps, some failure. When defeat overtakes a man, the easiest and most logical thing to do is to QUIT That is what the majority of men do.

NAPOLEON HILL, *THINK AND GROW RICH*

(If you're unfamiliar with Mr. Hill or his work, *Think, and Grow Rich*, was published in 1937. Since then, millions of people have credited its contents for helping them find success. The book's first principle is that to be successful, you need to have a burning desire backed by a definite purpose, not passion. I'm a big believer in *Think and Grow Rich* and would recommend it to anyone with an entrepreneurial spirit).

James 2:20 says, "Faith without works is dead," meaning that if you have a desire for something but don't act on it—it doesn't matter how much you yearn for it or believe it will come to pass; if you don't allow yourself to go through the process, you'll never achieve it.

RISE ABOVE THE NOISE

Noises, in this context, are those things that will fill your ears (and mind) with sounds to muffle, distract, or silence the authentic voice in your head. The noise comes in many forms, such as dissension, generational traditions, unforeseen setbacks, and people who care about you telling you not to start your business because, after all, you don't have a business degree.

The goal of my parents' generation, and many in my generation (because it was handed down to us), was and is to find a good job, stay there for 30 years, get your 401K, and retire at 65 or older with a pension. Nod your head if you've heard it before— it's okay if you're on a subway surrounded by strangers; nod your head anyway and agree with me. My parents tried to pass it on to me. I tried it; I truly did. However, it was like trying to fit a square peg in a round hole.

Based on my experience, I believe that most of the time they're sharing out of pain or fear. I believe that their advice and some-times admonishments are not to hurt you...they are meant to protect you from the possibility of the pain and discouragement of failure. So, the next time that you encounter this short-sided perspective of your plans, passions and purpose, feel free to use my quote, "I can live with losing the good fight. However, I could not live with myself if I did not attempt the fight at all."

Every time I would find a good job, somehow (I say it was God), it would become uncomfortable for me. It was like I was an oyster, and the uncomfortableness at my jobs would irritate me, as does a grain of sand that enters an oyster and makes it uncomfortable. Like many uncomfortable "oysters," I finally had enough, and when we realized the entrepreneurial life was for us, we came out as priceless pearls. I had to rise above the noise of people who cared for me. I had to limit access to me from people I cared for but were unknowingly trying to get me to quit on my goals.

Have you ever seen a bucket full of live crabs? It's fascinating, albeit infuriating. Whenever a crab on top would find a way to get out of the bucket, a crab below would grab it with its pincers and pull it back into the bucket. Maybe the lower crab is looking for a hand up, but what it is doing is holding back the higher crab over it, making it impossible for it to find its freedom next. Family and friends are just like that. It's infuriating!

I parallel this concept with the children of Israel coming out of Egypt, where they had been enslaved for 400 years; we're talking generations. First, they lived in The Land of Not Enough as slaves. Generations of people lived in that land, not having enough but willing to stay there because it was all they knew, and being free would be too much of a risk.

Then, Moses came to the scene, and they left Egypt and entered The Land of Just Enough. They had just enough, but at least they were making it on their own. They didn't have their territory yet, they were walking aimlessly, but they weren't enslaved anymore. This could be someone getting a degree, a vocation, an apprenticeship, taking real estate investment courses, watching YouTube videos on drop-shipping, or starting a side hustle on weekends. You have just enough, but you're not where you're destined to be.

I want you to come to the realization with me that God gave you The Land of More Than Enough. However, you must be willing to go through the journey, the desert—the process. Then, once you get there, you must work to stay there! Becoming a champion is a one-time event. If you don't train harder than ever, you'll never become a defending champion.

I leave this chapter with these two nuggets:

1. Don't just suffer through the process; find a way to enjoy it. Delight in the little wins; it'll make the process much more enjoyable.
2. You can't silence the noise because you're not the one making it. Find the inner resolve to rise above it.

CHAPTER 5
A GROWTH MINDSET

 "The universe does not award anyone the gifts of lifelong success.

They have to be earned over and over again.

Joy and fulfillment are moving targets,

as are health and wealth."

GARY T. HARTFIELD

SUCCESS IS NOT A ONE-TIME EVENT

At this point, I hope you have searched within yourself and have defined what success looks like for you. If you haven't, you have time now—put this book aside and picture the life you desire. Then, write it down. After all, in the Bible, God said to write the vision and make it plain. I promise, the book won't disappear; it'll be here when you're done.

Okay, take two.

At this point, you have searched yourself and have defined what success looks like for you. There are a few caveats to obtaining goals, though, that you need to be mindful of. When you reach your goal, be ready to create a new, bigger one! Success is not a one-time thing; it is the manifestation of repeated actions. Becoming a heavyweight champion is a one-time thing, but becoming a defending champion and a legend in the sport requires continued training and sacrifice. If your goal is to be the heavyweight champ and you rest on your laurels, the next up-and-coming fighter who also wants to be a champion will take your belt.

Remember, success is never given to one individual in perpetuity; once achieved, it needs to be protected and added to.

"SUCCESS IS NEVER GIVEN TO ONE INDIVIDUAL IN PERPETUITY"

Reaching one's life goals is a beautiful thing. But what will you do tomorrow, the next week, the next month, and in two years? I urge you to cultivate a growth mindset. Constantly look for new opportunities to acquire knowledge, whether it is through books, podcasts, conferences, training, or conversations with people with more specialized knowledge than you. The people who are happier and more fulfilled continue to expand their knowledge.

Beware the plateau. Beware the comfort zone. Beware of being content with social media likes and physical pats on the back. Having said that, if your goal was to be married with three children, and you're married with three children, I'm not saying to have a fourth. What I am saying is that now that you have those three children you wanted, find out how to make them more effective, better communicators, less shy, and human beings with integrity. Just because you have your three children doesn't mean the trying is done; now it's time to pivot and learn more so you can teach them more.

Those who stop learning start having diminishing returns. Will you have met your goals if two out of your three kids go to prison for life? It's never time to stop working, even if you have met your goals. The world passes by those who stop learning.

If you married your best friend and soulmate and are incredibly happy in your marriage, keep working on yourself and the marriage. If you decide binge-watching shows or YouTube videos is the best way to use your spare time, but your spouse continues their studies and gets a Ph.D., will you still have similar interests? What you once had in common can grow into a massive chasm that your love doesn't have enough fuel to cross. Many divorces don't happen because one person falls out of love with the other person; they happen because the other person gets lazy. They lost their curiosity for life or their partner. This opens the door for the enemy to come in and kill, not only their personal relationships, but also their spiritual and professional lives.

I got my undergrad in electronic engineering. It wasn't easy, and I felt the deck was stacked against me, but I persevered and reached that goal. I was proud of myself; I was the first in my family to earn a bachelor's degree. However, getting the degree wasn't the end goal; all that did was get me into the game. Now, I had to step up, study the marketplace, and play well. How technology works in electronics has evolved in many ways. I couldn't use the knowledge I gained to pass my tests in college after a few short years. I had to evolve with the technology to stay relevant.

THREE WAYS TO CULTIVATE A GROWTH MINDSET

Manage your associations. Managing associations involves recognizing the importance of humility and the need for continuous growth. The adage "the loudest one in the room is always the weakest one in the room" underscores the value of quiet confidence and active listening over brash self-promotion. It reminds us that true strength lies in understanding and leveraging the strengths of others rather than dominating conversations. Similarly, the saying "if you're the most successful person in the room, then you are in the wrong room" highlights the necessity of seeking environments that challenge and inspire personal and professional development. Surrounding oneself with individuals who are more accomplished fosters an atmosphere of learning and ambition, driving continuous improvement and preventing complacency. Thus, effective management of associations involves a balance of humility, active listening, and a relentless pursuit of growth by choosing the right company.

Find ways to get into new conversations. Look for those who have what you seek and penetrate that person's circle. Surround yourself with those who celebrate your wins and hold you to a high standard when you're not at your best.

Be a lifelong learner. You don't need to practice everything you learn, but be open to learning everything. The Bible says to examine everything but only hold fast to what is good. You don't have to become a drug user to study its effects and be able to help someone who has a drug problem. The knowledge you gain is half for you and half for those whose paths are destined to cross with yours.

Share your knowledge. If I learn a profound truth from a book, I'll share it with someone I think can benefit. Our relationship then changes immediately. Together, we have grown in wisdom on a particular subject and can help each other get to a higher level in that area. If you manage your associations correctly, the law of reciprocity will manifest and your inner circle will share life-enhancing knowledge with you!

Set Goals. It is crucial that you find what you want to accomplish in life. Allow me to share with you how to set goals properly. First, you come to terms with yourself and find the desire God put in your heart. I've heard that called the BHAG—Big Hairy Audacious Goal. However, if that's your only goal, you'll have a tough time reaching it. Examine the journey or steps or levels you need to get to in order to reach that BHAG. Those are your smaller, easier-to-obtain goals. Write those out, too!

Something inside of you needed to change in order for you to reach that small goal. Getting there allowed you to accumulate a level of insight, knowledge, and wherewithal that you didn't have before. Now, as you embark on the next, smaller goal en route to your Big, Hairy, Audacious Goal, you have a deeper breadth of knowledge about what it takes and yourself, and it will make getting to that next goal easier. When you reach that next goal, you'll have re-equipped yourself with, not only more knowledge, but an added sense of confidence because you are progressing towards your BHAG. You might even be ready to help someone else get to their first small goal.

Now, this part is very important. Don't wait to celebrate. Just because you haven't reached your BHAG doesn't mean you shouldn't be proud of your accomplishments. Recognize your achievements and celebrate the small wins! You may not be at your destination of 10,000 steps but give yourself a fist-pump and an ice cream for walking the first 1,000. This will ensure that you enjoy the process, making it harder for you to quit and settle for less than you are capable of.

As with most things, there are levels to this. Yes, celebrate small wins, but also practice delayed gratification. Don't let the small wins overshadow the long-term goals. For example, you don't have to double your expenses just because you've doubled your income. It's not time to buy that latest Mercedes G Wagon and the million-dollar home just yet. You might fool yourself into thinking that you're doing well enough and let your true goal wither and die, or worse yet, you may not be able to maintain the payments of the new purchases and end up worse off than where you started.

I asked God to grant me the talent and specialized skills to develop real estate assets worth $10 million within 20 years. As I reached smaller goals and learned from others and my own experiences, I realized a way to expedite my journey to success. At one point, I had more than $2 million worth of equity in real estate. I realized I could leverage that to buy a $5 million property! Had I used the equity I had acquired, as some suggested, I would have never been able to leverage it for 150% more of what I had.

By exercising delayed gratification, I put myself in the position that if I needed a $400K injection, I could use OPM—Other People's Money to get it and leave my savings alone. The bank would do its property appraisal and due diligence and see the equity I had in other properties, so they financed the $400K and held $400K in collateral on the equity I had in other properties so that if anything terrible should happen to me, they get their money back. I would have never gotten to that position if I had used up the equity as soon as it was available.

Remember, set your Big Hairy Audacious Goal, whatever it may be, but also set the smaller goals along the way.

OVERCOMING LIMITATIONS

The first step in overcoming limitations is to recognize them. Take the time to consistently assess where you are and the roadblocks keeping you from the next level. Then, find out if it's in your power to solve the problem. If it's a knowledge issue, learn it; if it's a timing issue, be patient but diligent in preparing to be ready when the time is right; if it's a credit issue, fix your credit.

In the Bible, we find that Moses knew his limitations—he stuttered. His ability to articulate wasn't on par with those he needed to communicate with. I think Moses thought, *But God, how can I be YOUR mouthpiece when I can't even talk right?* To which God answered, "Moses, the purpose I gave you will bring you further than your limitations can hold you or your potential can bring you."

You may be reading this right now thinking, *but MY limitations are different.* Allow yourself to be free from that negative, limiting thought. People who came from worse than you, who had less than you, had more physical impediments than you, have broken the cycle of poverty for themselves and their families, and have lived the lives of their dreams. Trust me, you are not the heavyweight champion of sad, woe-is-me stories. You're not the person who has ever had it worse than any other human being who changed their destinies.

I had my share of limitations, and when I grew in wisdom, I realized I used them as excuses. My parents didn't go to college. They were not what I would call, financially literate. Yet, for me to get to where I wanted to be, I had to detach myself from their experiences and live 100% with the talents God gave me.

"WHILE MY MOTHER WASN'T A BOOK-SCHOLAR OR A MILLIONAIRE, SHE WAS WISE ENOUGH TO INSTILL IN ME THAT I COULD DO ANYTHING WITH GOD'S HELP BUT FAIL."

While my mother wasn't a book-scholar or a millionaire, she was wise enough to instill in me that I could do anything with God's help but fail. So, as I shattered myths and the limitations of my surroundings, my confidence in God and myself continued to grow.

Understand this profound truth: whatever your heart desires is what you are capable of having. If you can hold it in your head, and if you're bold enough to go for it, you can hold it in your hand one day. Just remember to always feed your growth mindset. The bigger it gets, the bigger your dreams get, the bigger legacy you leave for others to follow.

CHAPTER 6
THE HERO'S JOURNEY

STORYTELLING

Everyone is the protagonist of their own story, the star of the show or the main character of the movie of their lives. Now, if the movie is an adventure, comedy, or a sad tearjerker depends on your mindset. Still, the fact remains; you're the main star—the hero.

Storytelling has been going on ever since the days of Adam and Eve. It has been enhanced and studied and now, nearly perfected. Meaning, if someone were to weave a story the correct way, it's sure to be entertaining. Jason Campbell became famous for taking a monomyth—a template that shows the hero's journey common in many myths, folktales, and religions—and breaking down each segment of the journey. He broke it down to 17 different stages. However, I'm going to simplify it for you by sharing with you only what you need to become a hero.

Being that you are your own hero, and I believe you are on the path to success, I'm going to highlight the hero's journey for you so that, regardless of where you may find yourself, you'll see that you are on the right track. The very fact that you are taking time out of your day to read this and get this knowledge into your spirit and mindset proves you are on the right track!

We all go through the hero's journey. It's up to you if the hero is going to win or lose. No matter your personal experience, the country you live in, your socio-economic status, how many siblings you've had, if your mother died giving birth to you or if she's an amazing grandmother to your children, you are on your journey.

Sadly, too many people are too busy making excuses about oppression, discrimination, lack of access to capital or specialized knowledge, or whatever they allow themselves to believe to quit on themselves. Part of the reason I wrote this book is because too many heroes are not acting heroic, but maybe it's because they don't know how—allow me to shed light on the journey. Before I get into it, know this, the hero's journey is evolutionary. You don't go through it just one time. As soon as you feel you've become the hero, a new journey with the same trials and tribulations await. Sure, they are harder trials, but it's commensurate to the experience and strength you've gained from previous journeys.

THE CALL TO ADVENTURE

This call is the moment you realize you have to identify your purpose. It's similar to an awakening in your subconscious or spirit. A sudden realization enters your being that you are meant for more or that something is wrong that you are meant to make right. In the smash hit, *The Matrix*, distributed by Warner Brothers Pictures in 1999, our hero, Neo intrinsically knew something was wrong. He had no data, no revelation, no huge discovery—it was an unsettling feeling.

The call to adventure is an internal call. Far too often, people wait for someone to see something in them and tell them what their purpose is. In church, people close their eyes praying for the preacher who doesn't know them to call their name out of the blue and tell them their purpose (God's plan for them). That's not how it works. An external force isn't going to write it on a wall that you accidentally walk by.

In my experience, it was an internal stimulus that I couldn't resist. What I wanted didn't make sense, no one in my family had done it, no one modeled it for me, and I wasn't born with superpowers. How could I not just think or hope, but expect to be wildly more successful than anyone else I had known at the time? But it didn't have to make sense to anyone else, including me—I had heard the call and set out on an adventure.

I urge you to embrace your life as I'm depicting it—an adventure. If you allow yourself to view life that way, you will understand that coming up short is part of the process and you wouldn't get so down on yourself when it happens. Life is beautiful. Life is amazing. Embrace it as the adventure it is and enjoy it, regardless of where and how today finds you. Your adventure is not over, tomorrow is just past the horizon, and you'll have another crack at it. Answer the call and get back to it!

THE CROSSING OF THE FIRST THRESHOLD

This stage of the journey emerges after the hero has heard the call to adventure (realized what his or her purpose is) and has now crossed from thinking about it to taking the first action. It could be leaving the small town you always lived in or delving into an unknown, far from your comfort zone and into a place where the rules and limits are unknown. It could be as easily as letting people know about your plans, creating a vision board, writing a business plan, writing your goals, or recruiting someone to help you.

While some may think this is the most insignificant part of the journey, I would counter that it's the most important because a journey can never end if it never starts. Sharing with your spouse about the greatness within you takes courage. Leaving a comfortable job for a dream takes courage, even if it's setting the date when you'll leave the job and you start putting in place what's needed for you to resign.

Most people are enslaved by the safety net called a job. The comfort zone of a steady paycheck has robbed more dreams than drugs, alcohol, or lack of a formal education. Realizing your call, your purpose is an internal phenomenon, but crossing the first threshold is an exterior act. It sets the dominos up for what's about to transpire.

Mentorship and Trials. Morpheus assumed the role of a mentor, guiding Neo through the challenges he faces within the Matrix. In the movie, *The Black Panther*, Zuri, portrayed by Forest Whitaker, serves as a spiritual and wise figure in T'Challa's life. Zuri plays a vital role in introducing T'Challa to the ritual and traditions of Wakanda. Without Zuri's guidance, T'Challa would have never gained the powers of the Black Panther.

As I said when I started this book, you will have trials. Every hero has at least one. Don't cry if you suddenly find you have haters; they've hated on you all along, you're now doing enough that they express their opinions about you. If you don't have haters, it's because you aren't doing anything.

During the trials is usually when that voice in your head starts to whisper to you that you can't succeed. You have put things in motion and you're going through the motions but in your heart of hearts you're having doubts. This is when you feel like a fraud, commonly known as Imposter Syndrome. You feel like you're fooling yourself and others to believe you could ever get to your goal.

Let me tell you something about Imposter Syndrome; it's a bully. It will try to beat you up and take your lunch money. If you allow it to go unchallenged your journey will end there—the tragic hero. Here's the thing about bullies; they like easy prey. If you fight against it, and even if you lose to it, it will question if it wants to fight you again. Too many people don't know the secret of beating their bullies because they can't beat their bullies up. Beating it isn't the only option in dismissing it—just fight it.

Fight the thoughts that you bit off more than you can chew.

Fight the feeling that you're not equipped to finish the journey.

Fight the feeling of being overwhelmed and slow down and just focus on the next thing you need to do, not all the things you need to do.

Fight the vision in your mind of people laughing at you, of hearing a family member saying they were right about you, of your kids seeing you fail. Take control of the vision you have for yourself of you winning, of your child seeing you get knocked down but getting back up.

A trial is not a dead end. It's just another challenge to beat. Let the trials come—you have a mentor and you're a hero.

Abyss and Revelation. There is ncwhere in your journey that you'll get as much revelation as when you are in the abyss. My descent into the abyss came swiftly. I had passed many trials. I was a father, a black male, with an undergraduate degree in engineering and a master's degree in business. I was newly married and just started my business. I thought my trials were behind me and soon would come the rewards.

Then came the grief of losing my sister and business partner. Then, I got laid off and was not able to find employment in a tough job market. I had the degrees, but I couldn't feed them to the family to keep us fed. After looking at my prospects a sense of fear and despair smacked me. The only job I saw that I could get immediately was to join the Day Labor pool. My wife was in tears when I told her. She had the highest of hopes when she married me—a confident, well-spoken man with all the education required to be successful. Yet, she couldn't find the potential she had seen in me.

I will say that every human being has pride. Yet, to provide for my family, I put whatever pride I had aside when I woke up at 4 AM and drove to a construction site. Gone were the suit, tie, shoes, and briefcase. On that day I wore boots, tough jeans, and an old sweatshirt mostly hidden by a bright yellow vest. We lived in Sanford, and I was being sent to Orlando in the cold to hold the cones and stop signs so that traffic could safely get around the construction site. I had hit rock bottom. However, I didn't have time to be prideful or to cry. I needed to do what it took to get paid.

However, some people will always see you for who you are meant to be. When I walked into the construction site trailer, it was plain on their faces what they thought when they saw me: *Why are YOU here?*

I put on my big-ole smile, said good morning and asked where they were sending me. The guy in front of me didn't have it in him to send me out in the cold. "Ummm," he stammered. "There was a mix up, we don't have work for you today."

"Are you sure? I was just speaking to someone yesterday and…"

"Sir, there has to be a million other places you can work. I'm sorry, we don't have anything for you today."

I called my wife, who also got up early to drop me off, to turn around and pick me up before she went to work. Had they sent me out, I would have done the best job I could to hold that stop sign and allow traffic to drive smoothly by for the entire day. I gained another muscle that day—I proved to myself that I would do whatever it took to provide for my family.

The revelation came to me that I became much more dangerous to whatever stood in the way of reaching my goals. It was then that the words spoken by my mother all of my life became a truth. "Gary, don't you know God will never bring you this far to leave you?"

I had answered, "Mom, there can't be a god that would allow me to be in this situation in the first place." Doubt in the abyss is real.

She answered, "That's because you're confused with the time. God won't respond to you in YOUR time, He'll do it in HIS time, which will be ON time." Those words took root and, as proof, my children have heard those words over and over again.

You may not be successful the first time, Hero. You may lose the house, the business may go bankrupt, and, most likely, you'll uncover that you have some destructive idiosyncrasies and vulnerabilities you need to address. You even may find yourself worse off than when you started. It's okay. It's part of the process.

The abyss is where you find your metal and character. Everything else is stripped away and you're finally getting to know you—without distractions.

Being in the Abyss, in the Valley of the Shadow of Death, you'll come to terms with the best of you and your faith. Just know this; God's plan is for you to get through in the abyss, not die in it. Keep walking, hero.

> "BEING IN THE ABYSS, IN THE VALLEY OF THE SHADOW OF DEATH, YOU'LL COME TO TERMS WITH THE BEST OF YOU AND YOUR FAITH."

<u>Transformation and Atonement.</u> The more you get through trials, the more you'll transform. Soon, you'll find yourself in a place that the "old" you couldn't handle, but that the transformed you will handle with ease. Remember this very important piece of this puzzle; there is no transformation for those who quit.

A newfound belief system emerges in the hero—a belief in him or herself. You have accepted that you're a work in progress and now appreciate the process even more. You have seen unseen forces work in your favor (I call him God). You have seen family walk away but you've partnered with strangers who respect you more and work with you easier. You transform into someone who believes anything can happen and the things that do happen do so for you and not against you.

<u>Return and Integration.</u> This is the final stage of the Hero's Journey. It involves the return to the ordinary world, armed with newfound wisdom and abilities. In "The Matrix," Neo returns to the Matrix to confront the agents and challenge the established order. In the same way, you'll look at the world around you with the certainty that you have the power to change what you don't like about your life and the skills and experience to live the life you were meant to.

Then, as you start your next journey to bigger and better things, you turn around and become a mentor for those who are where you were and want to go where you are. You find that you must find the time to share and empower others.

John C. Maxwell has a great quote that resonates with me:

"If you want to learn something, read about it. If you want to understand something, write about it. If you want to master something, teach it."

It doesn't matter what you look like, how old you are, or where you live—you have the power and ability to become the hero your family needs. Embrace the call of adventure, cross the first threshold, find a mentor and take on the trials, go through the abyss and find your revelation, be transformed and seek to atone for whatever you may have not done correctly, then return to do it all over again, while teaching others how you did it.

If you need just one person to believe in you, I'll give you two. God and me. You were made for more, go get it.

CHAPTER 7
CONFIDENCE. THE FOUNDATION FOR LASTING SUCCESS

DEFINING SELF-CONFIDENCE

Confidence, like success, is not a place that you arrive at and remain indefinitely. Confidence is like a muscle. It must be exercised and properly cared for to sustain it.

I define confidence as the emotion or belief derived from personal experience of overcoming trials, tribulations, and setbacks. Only by living through numerous battles can one accrue the unshakable, palpable, and immutable spirit to believe in oneself that, regardless of the circumstances, one will triumph and move forward. Confidence must be birthed somehow-somewhere; otherwise, it's foolish arrogance.

History is filled with people who not only had courage and ability, but also unwavering confidence. Abraham Lincoln is certainly among this group. He became the President of the United States of America when it was still figuring out who she needed to be. The nation had 33 states in its union, but a terrible moral divide afflicted it. Lincoln had the confidence to make a decision that would ultimately provoke a civil war that would claim many lives. Yet, he knew that the institution of slavery was not sustainable if America were to attain long-term success and prosperity. He had the confidence to abolish it then and there, regardless of how bad things would get, for the betterment of the country and all her people.

Harriet Tubman is another historical figure who possessed unshakable confidence. After escaping her entire life as an enslaved person, she made 13 life-risking missions and rescued hundreds of enslaved people, including her family and friends. In 1858, she teamed up with John Brown and helped him plan and recruit supporters for the 1859 raid on Harper's Ferry, where an estimated 700 slaves were freed.

The country was inhabited by many abolitionists (people who wanted the enslaved people freed), but most never risked their own lives to make it happen. Standing at five feet even, Harriet had the confidence to return again and again to the South, where she would have been hung if caught, to free as many slaves as she could. Her numbers would have been higher had some known they were enslaved at all. The slaves of that time were born into that cruel world and that was the only world they knew. They had no idea that African Americans in the North and Canada were free people or that it was an option if they were willing to fight for it.

It can be confusing, at times, to distinguish the purposeful manner in which a person walks, their gait, between confidence and arrogance. Both give off the illusion of a self-assured person. However, both characteristics are as opposite as the North and South were during America's civil war. To me, having confidence is believing that a higher power (God) has given me the ability and favors me to do the work of my hands. Arrogance assumes you can and will do everything with your wit and power.

Both seeds produce vastly different fruits. Confident leaders are able and willing to duplicate what they have done. They search high and low for other candles to light. They are lovers of the abundance mindset and know that allowing others to shine does not diminish their own shine. On the other hand, the fruits of arrogance are loneliness and fear of competition because it is based on a scarcity mindset. They don't share their secrets. Their actions say, *"Nobody helped me; you'll have to figure it out for yourself, too!"* Their sole belief in just themselves limits their effectiveness and makes them vulnerable to confident leaders.

BUILD CONFIDENCE THROUGH ACTION

Nothing is ever accomplished by staying paralyzed by fear. You must take the first step beyond what you know and recognize that there is an exterior, all-powerful force that will help you navigate murky waters. The operative word is action. You can only be confident if you take action.

You may be among the millions of Americans who have considered writing a book. Perhaps you have taken a writing class or course, and you've discussed with close friends the idea of your book—all of whom, by the way, told you it was a great idea. Yet, fast forward to 5, 10, or 20 years, and the book is still just an idea because you never put any action behind it.

Two types of energies are described in the world of physics: potential and kinetic. Potential energy is heard but only sometimes seen. It's when someone talks about something but doesn't put any action behind it. It's all hype but no substance. Kinetic energy is motion. It's taking the potential and putting it to the test. If you're not doing something, you're all talk, no action. Your legacy will be as frail and thin as the book idea in your imagination.

You may think to yourself:

Okay, I get it; it's time to take action. But:

What if I stumble?

What if I try and fail?

How would I build confidence through failed actions?

I would answer those thoughts in two ways:

THEODORE ROOSEVELT'S MAN IN THE ARENA

In Theodore Roosevelt's riveting quote about the Man in the Arena, he refers to the person who is actively involved in an activity or undertaking, despite the risk of failure or criticism. He uses the image of a gladiator fighting in an arena to illustrate the concept.

"It's not the critic who counts; not the man who points out how the strong man stumbles, or where the doer of deeds could have done them better. The credit belongs to the man who is actually in the arena, whose face is marred by dust and sweat and blood; who strives valiantly; who errs, who comes short again and again because there is no effort without error and shortcoming; but who does actually strive to do the deeds; who knows great enthusiasms, the great devotions; who spends himself in a worthy cause; who at best knows in the end the triumph of high achievement, and who at the worst, if he fails, at least he fails while daring greatly so that his place shall never be with those cold and timid souls who neither know victory nor defeat."

For context, the "Man in the Arena" are those men and women willing to take action to improve their circumstances and lives. Ask yourself, are you in the arena or are you still a spectator?

MICHAEL JORDAN, JK ROWLING'S, AND COLONEL SANDERS

MICHAEL JORDAN

It's okay if you don't succeed at first. The great ones usually don't. However, it's due to their failures or losses that they attribute their success. Michal Jordan, arguably the greatest basketball player ever, is quoted saying:

"I have missed more than 9,000 shots in my career. I've lost almost 300 games. 26 times, I've been trusted to take the game-winning shot and missed. I've failed over and over and over again in my life. And that is why I succeed."

In a YouTube video that surfaced in 2005 entitled, *Michael Jordan's Advice for Parents*, he says, and I'm paraphrasing, "When you take a shot, you can do one of two things: make it or miss. Teach that to your kids so they're not afraid of the simple act of taking their shot. When I would miss a shot, okay, tomorrow, I'm going to work hard to make sure that the next time I'm in the same situation, I can make the shot."

So, in the words of Michael Jordan—take action. Shoot your shot. If you fail, work hard and prepare to make it next time.

J.K. ROWLINGS

The last time J.K. Rowling's husband slapped her in the face was the last time he slapped her in the face. In addition to facing abuse, Rowlings' husband threw her out of their house, keeping their daughter Jessica. She later returned with police presence to retrieve her daughter and return to the U.K., along with the first three chapters of a book she intended to title *Harry Potter*.

With no place for her and her daughter to live, she moved in with her sister and brother-in-law. With no job and no job prospects, she applied for benefits and was able to rent a small apartment. She would later describe her predicament as "as poor as it is possible to be in modern Britain, without being homeless." She had hit rock bottom and struggled with continuous thoughts of suicide. She realized she needed to get herself together for her daughter if for no one else.

She went to therapy and began a one-year teaching training course. She completed her manuscript in 1995, just around the time she started looking for work as a teacher. She sent a three-chapter sample of Harry Potter and, to her delight, reeled in a London agent, Christopher Little. However, even with Christopher's help, the manuscript was received with rejection after rejection. After twelve rejections, Little landed a deal with Bloomsbury, a publishing house in London.

After many arguments with herself, she settled on the writer's name, "J.K. Rowling," because she was concerned about how males would respond to a female writer in that genre. Little did she know, it wouldn't matter.

Within just days of Harry Potter's debut, a children's publishing powerhouse named Scholastic bid more than $100,000 for the American publishing rights. They changed the name to Harry Potter and the Sorcerer's Stone, which took the United States and the world by storm. The highly successful sequel, Harry Potter and the Chamber of Secrets, followed a year later. Warner Bros signed on with a feature-film deal the following year.

The once, near homeless single mother who fled an abusive relationship became the first billionaire author in 2004. Rowling's never forgets her years of struggles; it is what fuels her future. She embraces the years of hardship of a single mother, much like the scar on the forehead of the character that made her so famous.

I added this story so that you know that no matter your story, you're still the author of your life. You, and only you, can define you. You, and only you, can write the following chapters of your life. I hope that excites you about your future.

COLONEL SANDERS

Colonel Harland Sanders embodied perseverance, ambition, and commitment. At sixty-five, when most adults didn't live past sixty-five, he found himself nearly penniless after running a restaurant for several years.

He retired and received his first social security check of a whopping $105. He realized that if he didn't do anything, he would die a pauper. After taking inventory of how he could sustain himself, he realized that he loved when people tried his fried chicken recipe. With little to no means at his disposal, Colonel Sanders traveled door to door to houses and restaurants. His goal was to partner with an established restaurant. Unfortunately for him, he was met with little enthusiasm.

He then traveled further, going as far as cooking his fried chicken on the spot for restaurant owners. He offered a handshake agreement: for each piece of chicken the restaurant sold, they would pay him a nickel. Legend has it that Colonel Sanders heard 1,009 "Nos" before he heard his first "Yes." Those who agreed were sent packages of his "secret recipe" so that it could remain a secret.

Did you get that? At the age of sixty-five, he was rejected 10, 20, 100, 500, 678, 899, 1,000, and 1,008 times before he landed his first deal!

His perseverance paid off. Not only did he stop getting a nickel for each chicken from his partners, but he opened his first Kentucky Fried Chicken restaurant—and by 1964, he had 600 franchise stores selling his trademark chicken. He then sold his company for $2 million with the condition that he remain its spokesperson. In 1976, he was ranked the world's second most recognizable celebrity.

A statue of his likeness can be found all the way on Nathan Road in Kowloon, Hong Kong.

I add Colonel Sander's story here because you may feel that time has passed you by or the opportunity of your lifetime has passed you by. Success doesn't cater to age. The chance to be successful doesn't just swing around once in a lifetime.

DARE

Dare to dream that you can live the life you want. As Jordan said, take your shot. Open that business. Take out that loan. Invest in that property. Ask her out on that date. Don't be too proud and ask for help. Do it with confidence. As Rowlings kept writing her story during the worst time in her life, don't let one part of your life rob you of the confidence to act in other areas of your life. As Colonel Sanders did, eat up and spit out any rejections or thoughts of rejections and keep pushing.

You're a battleship. Not only are you built for storms, but you also have God-given weaponry at your disposal. Take your shot with confidence. If you miss it, it's okay. Reload and take another. Whatever you do, make sure you leave with your guns empty when you leave this world. If you do, you will have lived an admirable and confidence-filled life.

CHAPTER 8
THE POWER OF POSITIVE TALK

WHAT'S YOUR B.S.?

In numerous chapters, I've shared the importance of surrounding yourself with the right people. It is, and always has been, one of the core ingredients in the recipe for success. Now that I've established that principle, let's go deeper, shall we?

It is vital to surround yourself with the right people, but the fact remains that whoever you surround yourself with is not with you every second of every day. Even for married people, not even your spouse is around you every second of every day. However, there is someone who is always there. That person, dear reader, is you.

I need you to understand that you are either your biggest enemy or biggest cheerleader in the form of what you believe, or to put it in a more popular term, Your Belief System.

What you believe has as much to do with what happens to you than any single other thing, including the all-mighty God, because God ordained it that way when he granted you free will. Your free will has brought you through experiences, many of which were out of your control as a child and growing up, but it also gave you choices once you had a say over what you said and did.

Dr. Milton H. Erickson is known as a psychotherapy innovator. His unique techniques and approaches have paved the way for modern therapy. He was so respected that he is long considered the father of modern clinical hypnosis. He was so impactful to his patients that they named his methods after him: Ericksonian Therapy and Ericksonian Psychotherapy. Although he passed away in 1980, nearly 100 Erickson institutes exist in almost 30 countries.

After working with tens of thousands of patients in his more-than 30-year career, he concluded that **85% of what you expect to happen…will.**

What you expect comes from a deeper place than your thoughts. It comes from your subconscious thoughts. In other words, it comes from your Belief System.

Subconsciously, if you believe that you'll never be wealthy because your conscious brain tells you that no one in your family has been wealthy, if you believe that you'll never be in great shape because your conscious brain tells you that your family has a history of illnesses, that you'll never graduate college because your conscious brain tells you that no one from your family or from where you came from went to college, that you'll never be an entrepreneur because no one in your family has ever owned a business—all of those things will or will not happen. You'll never be wealthy, you'll never be in great shape, you'll never be a college graduate, and you'll work for someone else your entire life without ever opening a business.

You may read this and think: *I can't help it. I've been ingrained to think this way, and my limiting thoughts have filtered into my subconscious mind; even though I know I can do more with my life, my belief system is limited. What can I do?*

That, my friend, is why I wrote this book. To get you unstuck, first with your faith, then within your mind, and get you ready to take over the world.

Here's the answer that has the authority to change your life: Release the Power of Positive Talk!

POSITIVE TALK

Our fears come to us without permission. We don't sit down, have a coffee, and start a list of things we want to be frightened of. It doesn't work like that. Our fearful thoughts come unbidden. Even though they are unwelcome, no one has the power to stop them. It's a part of the human experience. However, just because you can't prevent them from entering your mind doesn't mean you are powerless. It is 100% up to you if you entertain those thoughts or cast them out.

One way to fortify yourself from debilitating thoughts lingering in your brain for so long that they settle into your subconscious is utilizing the power of Self-Talk. We can't help the thoughts that come to our minds, but when we speak, we do it with intentionality.

Things to say to yourself:

I'm better than this.

I'm going to do something great today.

I'm the head, not the tail.

I can do all things through Christ Jesus who strengthens me.

I'm not scared of what people may say; I've got to do me.

My family deserves the best version of me.

I deserve the best version of myself.

I may be in this position now, but today, I initiated the process to get to a better position.

Today, I continue on the path of sobriety.

Then, use something to remind you of what you told yourself. For me, it was keeping things in front of me. My house was littered with sticky notes and poster notes. I had some on my bathroom mirror, on my computer, by the bed, in my bible, and in other areas I would consistently see. The reminder of who God made me to be was constant. Even though I came from very humble beginnings, my belief system shifted to believing that God had deposited more in me than I was utilizing.

Constant, positive, affirmations and reminders are essential to your success journey. That's how the world of advertising works. Billion-dollar companies don't just buy one ad and expect everyone to use their product. They purchase multiple ads on multiple channels—television, social media, radio, podcasts, and billboards. It's often the same message, over and over again, until we know their jingle or slogan. They know that once we know their jingle by memory, when the time comes to buy a product they sell, we will buy it from them because it has reached our subconscious level, and WE TRUST THEM.

In the same way, bombard yourself with positive talk and reaffirm it with imagery that will keep you true to who you said you would become. Just as you trust these big brands, even if you don't know anyone who works there, TRUST YOUR FUTURE SELF, even though you have yet to become that person.

Don't underestimate the power of repetition. Top-tier athletes practice the same moves hundreds of thousands of times, if not millions. Stephen Curry is arguably known as the best shooter to ever play in the NBA. I can't imagine how many 3-point shots he has taken over his lifetime in just practice. I can't imagine how many times Tiger Woods has rocketed a golf ball off a tee. I can't imagine how many punches Mike Tyson has thrown into the air. I'm sure the numbers are outrageous. Yet, it's through repetition that they perfect their skills. In the same way, repeat giving yourself positive self-talk and witness the metamorphosis on the ways you think, which will manifest into a change in your life.

Dr. Erickson went on to explain (and I'm paraphrasing here) that continually speaking positively of yourself becomes part of who you are. Also, the words don't disappear once the sound of your voice is gone. It gathers in your subconscious until you develop a reservoir of strength you can draw from, even when evidence in front of you goes contrary to what you've been saying. Much like a boxer deflects a jab, your powerful mind will deflect the current situation and not let it hurt you. You'll remind yourself that your current situation is only a temporary situation and that by continuing to work on yourself, you're headed to a better destination.

My mother shared with me, repeatedly, nothing but positive talk and how God is the one who has the last word—the same God that loves me and has plans of good for me, loves you and has good plans for you.

I heard it so often; it became a part of me. I no longer have to write some things down because it's part of my belief system. Now, I expect to win. I expect to come out on top. I expect to get offered lucrative partnerships. I expect that when something unexpected happens, it does so in my favor.

Self-talk doesn't only have to be voiced conversationally. It can also be written. As you know by now, I'm a huge believer in writing a business plan. The Bible says to write the vision and to make it plain. Write down your best life five years from now and read it often.

Self-talk can also be sung. In fact, the easiest way to remember words is through song lyrics. This is why, for me, worship music is so vital to not only my relationship with God but also my mood, my generosity, and the vision I have for my future.

Understand this—positive talk is not a one-time thing or something to abandon once you've manifested the items on your vision board. Self-talk is a lifelong conversation. You're always having it, whether or not you choose to engage in it. But if you're not, who's speaking for you? Stay vigilant and make sure always to be the driver on that you-bus. You choose where your brain goes, where your energy goes, and the legacy you're going to leave behind.

IMPOSTER SYNDROME

If you've never worked on yourself in the field of self-development, you've most likely not faced the hideous, powerful nemesis called Imposter Syndrome. It springs out of the crevices of your subconscious once you determine to become better—at anything.

For me, Imposter Syndrome started when I started to achieve positions in life defined by various versions of success. While I began to rise to levels that would even surprise me, I was having losing battles with personal vices. My Imposter Syndrome would attack my faith, my family, and the way the community perceived me.

You call yourself a man of God; why did you do X?

Oh, everyone thinks you're such a great husband and father, how about the knockdown drag-out yelling match you all just had?

If everyone really knew who you really are and what you're capable of...

I started questioning my integrity, values, reasons, and myself.

Am I working so hard so that people can look up to me? Am I seeking admiration?

If I'm such a good man, why do I have grievances with my ex-wife?

Am I not the person I think and say I am?

I was becoming successful in leaps and bounds in one area of my life but also questioning the fiber of my very being, wondering who I thought I was. However, God, as He always does, showed up right on time. He let me understand the fallacy of man and woman from the beginning of time when Adam and Eve fell. Sure, that didn't omit me from actions and deeds I needed to improve upon, but it did take away the guilt or shame the enemy tried to bury me in.

Your personal vice might be porn, talking behind someone's back, overeating, smoking weed daily, drinking too much alcohol, lying without even realizing it, stealing, coveting what others have, etc. I'm not saying to stay doing those things, what I'm saying is to give yourself the same grace God gives you.

This revelation helped me realize that I'm not an imposter. I'm a perfectly broken human, a descendant of the first man who is, despite my shortcomings, continually trying to better myself.

Free yourself from any past guilt. You have the power, this very moment, to alter the trajectory of your life. You may think you've been this way for too long, or you can't teach an old dog new tricks! Let me warn you—Beware of limiting beliefs!

Lose those loser-like thoughts. They'll keep you mired in mediocrity, or worse—poverty, for the rest of your life.

Adopt new mantras, such as:

A journey of a thousand steps starts with one step.

How do you eat an elephant? One bite at a time.

Rome wasn't built in a day.

Little by Little, a Little becomes A Lot!

You don't have to change everything in one shot. Just do a brief, one-degree pivot. That's all. If you did a one-degree pivot in the journey that is the rest of your life, imagine it to be 20,000 miles. That one-degree pivot can save you from freezing in the North Pole and, instead, basking under the glorious sun on the white sands of a beach in the Caribbean.

CHAPTER 9
CULTIVATING THE POWER OF HABITS: LAYING THE GROUNDWORK FOR ACHIEVEMENT

UNDERSTANDING HABITS

There's a famous saying that goes, *you are what you eat.* Have you heard it? I'm sure you have since it's been bantered around for more years than I can remember. The funny thing about popular sayings is that there is truth in them. However, as much as I understand what that saying means, I must disagree and counter with: *You are what you do.* Since what we do habitually is the most consistent thing, I will edit that statement to declare: *You are your habits.*

Wikipedia has a great definition of a habit: *A habit is a routine of behavior that is repeated regularly and tends to occur subconsciously.*

Over time, our individual experiences, combined with our need for safety, comfort, love, and acceptance, materialize in what we do and say. The repetition of these actions and words slips from our conscious (thinking) mind. It enters our subconscious (you don't even have to think about it) mind, and the actions and words continue to get expressed automatically. Once anything enters one's subconscious, it becomes incredibly powerful. It becomes a part of the essence of that person. That is why fewer things in life are more challenging to break than a habit. You are, dear reader, a representation of the habits you have formed.

Habits can be enabling or disabling; depending on which ones you cultivate. Regardless of your habits, you must know that you do what you do because, in some way, you believe it serves you, even the bad ones. Your habits become the embodiment and representation of you who are psychologically, spiritually, and physically to the world. Your habits and you are one and the same. Your whole being is based on the habits you've formed.

Habits are so powerful that they control what you will do tomorrow more than what you want to do tomorrow.

GOOD AND BAD HABITS

People who have cultivated good habits are, for the most part, happy, successful, loving, popular, accepted, trustworthy, and loyal. They don't even dare think of stabbing anyone in the back. They would never steal. Mostly, they take care of themselves physically, so they aren't sickly or sick often. They are contributing members of their families and society. They set high standards and make people around them better.

People who have cultivated bad habits are, for the most part, unhappy. They may be wealthy, successful, or popular, but regardless of whatever material possessions they may have or the status they achieve, internally, they are not happy with themselves. In most cases, though, people with bad habits are not wealthy, successful, or popular. They are constant complainers who try to convince themselves and others that things outside of their control are why they are not winning. They don't stand for anything, so they fall for everything. They want, desperately, to become better people, to incorporate new habits, but they have yet to be able to do so.

What most people with bad habits, or even an addiction, don't realize is that somehow, in some way, shape, or form, they believe their bad habit serves them in some capacity. Even though an alcoholic desperately wants to quit drinking, he or she doesn't because, in their subconscious, they believe it serves a purpose. Maybe it's to forget painful memories. Maybe because it just makes them feel good. Maybe it's their form of relaxation. Maybe they think they are better company, more outgoing, or more daring when they're drinking. They try to break the habit on the conscious level but will always be unsuccessful because, on a subconscious level, they want to drink.

This goes for every addiction and bad habit. However, you have an ally—and first and foremost, I say it's God. However, I know not everyone shares the same belief as me, so I'll say this—your ally is you!

Your inner voice also resides in your subconscious.

In order to break a bad habit, first, one must get in sync with one's inner voice. The problem is that there's often something to block you from hearing the voice. Ask yourself: *What is blocking me from listening to the voice in my head? It constantly warns or tries to guide me around pitfalls, yet I never adhere to it.*

"IN ORDER TO BREAK A BAD HABIT, FIRST, ONE MUST GET IN SYNCH WITH ONE'S INNER VOICE."

Allow me to share this easy-to-understand, yet incredibly powerful truth: There is only one YOU on this planet. There has never been a YOU before, and there will never be a YOU after. Stop living your life the way others think you should. Stop picking your career based on what others think you're good at. Stop dating the type of men and women popular culture says it's cool to be with. Stop going to those places with your friends you don't enjoy. Empower yourself to be who you want to be.

You can initiate change right now if you believe you can. Refer back to your purpose. Bury your *why* into your heart and mind. Are you really going to live your only life on earth being someone you'd rather not be? I have asked you numerous times to write things down as we've journeyed through this book. I hope you have. However, if you haven't, I ask you again to write down your purpose and your why. Write down all the things you do instead of doing the things that get you closer to your purpose. Write down why you do them instead of what you want to do. You need to know, for yourself, why it's so important to you. You can have a stadium full of people cheering for you, but if you don't help yourself, there's little anyone else can do.

Personal growth is not a rest area; it's more like a flowing river, an ongoing occurrence. You are continually growing one way or the other. Oh, and if anyone thinks that staying the same is not growing, they're wrong. Staying the same is you growing worse.

I've been asked several times, "Gary, how do you do all the things you do in one day?" First, I take it as a sincere compliment that people admire my work ethic. I own multiple businesses, I attend different board meetings, I work on serious projects, I'm involved in my church and community, I'm an attentive father, I work long hours, and at this moment of my life, I still find the mental capacity and creativity to work on this, my second book.

I no longer have to practice being disciplined. I have done it for so long that being disciplined has become an integral part of my persona. It has become a powerful habit for me.

Not too long from the time of this writing, I attended a two-day conference. It was a high-level event and required me to be "on" the entire time, even at the dinners afterward. In the meantime, I was running my businesses and ensuring our projects were on pace. Then, I rushed to change my clothes and picked up my son, got him something to eat, and took him to his basketball game, all the while talking to my team about the contents I wanted to discuss in this book. I created myself into the version of me that is happy being this productive. I'm living the life I wanted. Just as I did, you can, too.

REPLACING OLD HABITS WITH NEW ONES

There is truly one way to solve almost any problem. Apply this three-step process to the things you want to change in your life, and you'll have a different life. I'll cater these three steps to replacing bad habits with better ones.

1. Acknowledge all the habits you have.
2. Address the problematic ones.
3. Find a solution and be consistent.

Everyone has good and bad habits. Write down what yours are. Now, habits are not only what you physically do or don't do; it can also be how you react to adverse events. Do you respond with fear or anger? Search yourself for the answers that only you can find.

Pick out the ones that you'd like to change. WRITE THEM DOWN.

- *Now that I have my own business, I sleep in too often.*
- *I drink too much*
- *I smoke too much*
- *I overeat*
- *I curse too often*
- *I'm always looking for shortcuts rather than excellence*
- *I go to bed too late*

- *I play games on my phone too often*
- *I don't charge enough for my work*
- *I bite my fingernails wherever I go*
- *I say 'yes' to everything*
- *I have road rage*
- *I procrastinate*
- *I don't take time for myself*
- *I'm too much of a people pleaser*
- *I don't have a routine*
- *I don't take care of myself (Bad hygiene)*
- *I lie or exaggerate a lot*
- *I over-share (Not everything needs to be told to people)*
- *I talk too much*
- *I get defensive quickly*
- *I listen to respond instead of listening to understand*
- *I avoid conflict (and things get worse)*
- *I'm a hoarder*
- *I eat too much junk food or fast food*
- *I'm disorganized*
- *I say I speak my mind, but people tell me I'm rude*
- *I overthink things and then don't do them*
- *I dwell on the past*
- *I don't exercise*
- *I don't drink enough water*

Once you've written down your bad habits, write down the repercussions they bring to your life. Changing bad habits is difficult if you don't internalize how negatively it impacts you. This is where you'll find the strength to change them.

- *I don't exercise so I'm overweight. I get tired quickly. I have to take medication. I can't play with my grandkids.*
- *I'm a hoarder, so I have no room in the house. Every room is cluttered. Even things that are of no value to me anymore take up space in my house/apartment.*

- *I have road rage, so at any moment, just because someone makes me tap on the breaks, it ruins my mood, and if anyone is with me, I ruin their mood. I get so angry I can punch someone. Maybe one day I will get arrested or beat up.*
- *I smoke too much. I'm high all the time. I can't enjoy food, movies, or basically anything as much without weed.*
- *I'm disorganized, so every day has no structure. It makes me unreliable to others and to myself!*

Now, write down what you can do instead of doing those things. Just know that some habits will be easier to replace than others. Some habits have solutions, but others require willpower to quit cold turkey. However, with those, you can always find support.

- *Bad Habit: I don't exercise, so I'm overweight.*
- *Replace with:*
- *I will have a satisfying meal and stop eating after 8 PM.*
- *I'm going to walk a half hour a day.*
- *I'm going to replace junk food with fruits.*
- *Bad Habit: I dwell on the past*
- *Replace with:*
- *I will talk to a counselor, therapist, pastor, or trusted friend about it.*
- *I will plan what I'm doing next week, so I focus more on the future.*
- *If I find myself dwelling on the past, I will go to another room, turn to a different show, read a book—anything to change my frame of mind at that moment.*
- *Bad Habit: I go to bed too late*
- *Replace with:*
- *I will do some exercise so that I'm more tired at my desired bedtime.*
- *I will take a bath and drink some tea at 9 PM.*
- *I will shut the TV off and be off my phone by 9 PM.*

Replacing a habit doesn't always have to go head-to-head with the bad habit. There are things you can incorporate in the day that will automatically reduce the enticement or inclination to do the bad habit.

*For anyone struggling with an addiction, please consider speaking to a therapist or counselor.

THE POWER OF CONSISTENCY

Being consistent in not doing a bad habit or implementing a better one is the next vital step in breaking free from disabling habits. Golden State's Stephen Curry, an NBA Super star, is known as the greatest shooter in NBA history. If you don't take into account the game time, the 2-4 hours of team practice when not playing games, the hour-long shoot-around before games, and other athletic activities such as conditioning, lifting weights, and other exercises, he still finds time to put up hundreds of three-point shots per day. If you ask him why he's such a good shooter, in a word, he'd answer—consistency.

He has shot so many three-pointers during his life that he has a very good feeling about which ones are going in the basket and which are misses. Because of this, he has highlights of shooting the ball from the three-point range, turning around, and running back or turning to the opposing bench, as the ball is still in the air. As he's facing away from the basket, the ball swishes in. It might surprise many spectators but not him; he knew it was going in once it left his hand. How? Consistency.

Famous authors consistently write, famous athletes consistently train, and famous entertainers consistently practice. Those sports announcers you hear calling NFL games—they don't just call the games when it's game time; they watch video replays of prior games with their teams (fact checkers, media personnel, etc.) and practice by calling plays, even if it's with the help of a recording.

Being consistent is not limited to being productive in breaking habits; it's a vital key to success in every area of your life.

If you are an entrepreneur, you must consistently show up for yourself, your business, and your clients. You'll have a hemorrhaging business if you don't show up for those three parts consistently. If you're in customer service and want to be the best in your company, you need to provide tremendous value consistently.

Some people may not even try to break a bad habit because they feel they can't be disciplined forever. I've mentioned this already, but it's important enough that I'm writing this again—you don't need to be disciplined for the rest of your life. You just need to be consistent for 30 days. Then, the new habit will become your habit, and your old (disabling) habit will fade away. If you can harness the power of consistency for just one month, you can become the person you want to be.

AVOIDING TRIGGERS

People with bad habits tend to associate with others with similar habits. In order to break a disabling habit, you need to avoid the triggers that make it easier to do it. First, you have to identify that they exist. As I shared earlier in this chapter, the number one rule in changing something is to identify it.

If you're a smoker who works for a big company, you probably run outside during a work break and puff on a cigarette surrounded by other smokers. In their own way, smokers have developed their little slice of culture. Sometimes you brave the cold for that puff, occasionally the rain, sometimes the heat—but you all go at the same time every day. You would have a much better chance of quitting that habit if you didn't go outside with your friends while they smoked. It's perfectly within your right to establish protective boundaries.

"Sorry, man, I'm not going out there with you anymore."

"Come on. You don't have to smoke. It's not like I'm going to force you. I want to talk about the game last night."

"You don't understand; smelling it and watching people smoke makes me want to do it. If you're a real friend, you'll understand and never invite me to go with you again."

Those are the words of someone building himself or herself up to become unstoppable! Remember, a shared commonality can easily trigger you to do what you said you wouldn't. Instead of building up strength and confidence in yourself, you will consider yourself weak and not to be trusted, even by you! Those thoughts will settle into your subconscious, and you'll remain a smoker, maybe even after getting diagnosed with lung cancer. Yes, habits are that powerful!

REWARDS

Give yourself something to look forward to. Your mind and body will fight more for you if they know there is a reward coming if they can stand up to the pains of withdrawals. Maybe you treat yourself to a new outfit after just ten days of consistently going to the gym at the time you put on your calendar. Just as there are disabling triggers, there are enabling triggers.

Looking nice in a new outfit is a trigger. It releases endorphins through your body and confidence in your walk. Waking up without a hangover is an enabling trigger. Have that coffee with Jesus and start the day on a positive note. Getting a compliment is a trigger. It's not egotistical to enjoy or even work for a compliment. They are assurances that you are doing a good thing and that people notice.

You may have tried repeatedly to break a bad habit and have failed. It's okay. Steph Curry doesn't make every shot he takes.

He just keeps shooting. In the same way, nothing is stopping you from trying again. This time, however, take it more seriously. Use this chapter as a workbcok and write out the things I've asked. Examine how you have convinced yourself that your disabling habits somehow serve you. Challenge that rationale.

PUT IT TO THE TEST

There was a popular movie that came out in 2006 starring Gerald Butler called *300*. The backdrop is 480 B.C. The Persians, led by the God-King, King Xerxes, lead the world's largest and most powerful army. They try to subjugate the city-state of Sparta. However, the Spartan King, Leonidas (played by Gerald Butler), does not bend the knee and defies them.

Leonidas leads a small but seasoned group of warriors, 300 of them, to face a foe that can be seen for miles and miles. The Spartans forced the Persians to fight in a small enough area where they could not be outflanked; meaning, they could only meet their enemies head on, and the enemies couldn't throw their entire force on them at once. Hours of fighting turn into days and then, to everyone's surprise, weeks! Yet, the small, dwindling force of the Spartans still fought on.

This is why I tell you this story:

King Xerxes, frustrated of being thwarted by such a small force when compared to his, commands the deadliest battalion of the most powerful army. They call themselves immortals. This sets the stage for a saying I want you never to forget.

A tired, scared Spartan realizes who they are now up against. He says, "We are doomed. The child speaks of the Persian ghosts, known since ancient times. They are hunters of men's souls. They cannot be killed or defeated. Not this darkness. Not these Immortals."

King Leonidas, carrying the child's dead body the warrior referenced, says, "Immortals?" The camera pans in on him, and he says—and this is the saying: **"We will put that name to the test!"**

I share with you this bit of movie magic as a verbal illustration. You may have failed against disabling habits for as long as you remember. You might even think you'll never defeat it, that you'll do it to your dying day. That, in other words, those habits are 'Immortals' to your life.

But I tell you, dear reader, take a breath of new courage and say, "I will put that name to the test!" Continue fighting against your disabling habits. It can't beat you if you never quit. You are now better equipped than ever before.

CHAPTER 10
TIME MANAGEMENT AND THE POWER OF PRIORITIZATION

TIME

Lost somewhere in the epic movie, *The Hobbit,* is a riddle contest between Bilbo Baggins (our hero) and Gollum (one of the villains). It takes place deep under a mountain, amid shadows and gray light. Gollum does not know that Bilbo carries the one thing he wants more than anything, including his life—the One Ring, or as Gollum calls it, "My Precious." Bilbo has no idea that Gollum once had it and would kill for it.

The deformed creature Gollum is about to attack Bilbo, but Bilbo delays the attack by accepting a challenge of riddles.

The stakes:

If Bilbo wins, Gollum shows him the way out.

If Gollum wins, it eats Bilbo.

High stakes indeed!

I bring up this piece of movie magic to illustrate the power of my next topic. After a series of brilliant riddles being answered, to the dismay of both parties, the viewer gets a sense that someone is about to win and the other person is about to lose. That's when Gollum, who has been alive for more than 500 years, throws out his best riddle:

> *This thing all devours:*
> *Birds, beasts, trees, flowers;*
> *Grinds hard stone to meal;*
> *Slays kings, ruins town,*
> *And even beats high mountains down.*

Bilbo was running out of time and Gollum prepared to attack him again. Then, Bilbo's face lit up with a smile. He knew the answer.

"TIME!"

YOUR TIME

There is no living thing on the planet that will outlast time. It is infinite for those of us who are governed and measured by its passing. However, our physical bodies here on earth are finite. At best, we have 70, 80, or 90 good years. At worst, a surprise accident can take all the time in the world away in a split second. This is why, dear reader, realizing the value of time is so important.

You can't put a price on time. Ask any billionaire on their deathbed what's the one thing they would give their fortunes for. They'd answer: Time. However, they can't buy it. No one can.

It's a commodity that you can never get back. Once it's spent, it's gone forever. Every second is a once-in-a-lifetime event. You can never get back the time of your life you spent yesterday. What you can control, though, is how to leverage time so that you get a return on investing in it, meaning by doing things worthy of your values and goals so that as time continues its singular run, you are rewarded in a future time for what you do in the present time. That being said, make sure you're investing in time and not spending it.

A great way to invest time is to use it to get you closer to your goals or spend it with those you love. If your time is spent on people or the right projects, you'll be rewarded with the ROI (i.e., return on investment). Invest time by pouring into others, whether they are peers, family members, people in the community, admirers, students, or in a congregation. The fruits of your time in passing on wisdom and knowledge you've accrued through your studies or experience will be seen in others. That, my friend, is a beautiful way to live.

Time spent can be seen as driving an hour to a mall only to find out it has closed. That hour, and the hour drive back, cannot be recouped. It can't be repurposed. Like every other ticking second, that time is gone the moment that present turns into the past. Time disappears continuously and more time appears endlessly until you are out of time.

You can't negotiate with time and tell it, "Wait, I didn't mean to take that nap. Can I please get those 18 minutes back?" Nor can you barter with it; it needs nothing you have. Here's the most important thing you need to know about time: Don't worry about how much you have; instead, plan on how you're going to spend the time you have.

Some people think that binge-watching shows on Netflix is a waste of one's time. However, like everything else, it depends on the context. If you've been grinding on your goals and need to step back and binge on some Rom-Com or Sci-Fi or whatever entertains you—it's okay. For some, it's therapeutic. It's a form of using that time to recharge, to step out of the laptop, and allow other people's creativity to flood their vision and ears.

Now, if you replace working on your goals because you don't have the discipline to stop watching the entire 17 episodes of a show—you're wasting your time! I won't preach to you not to spend time on reels or TikTok videos. Why? Because it can be an inexpensive outlet to relieve stress. However, if you're on these or other social media sites instead of being present with your loved ones or doing that one super important thing you need to do today—know that you will reap what you sow into that time.

I'm not suggesting that you spend all your time, or allow your children to, spend all of their free time on social media. I am suggesting you be mindful of it, though. According to a Baylor University study, people's cell phones can be as addicting as heroin. Try taking the phone away from a 16-year-old in America and see the response you'll get. My point in sharing this, to the parents reading this, is first to moderate the time you spend on your phone (so that you show by example) and then moderate the time your children spend on theirs.

PRINCIPLES OF TIME MANAGEMENT

The single best thing you can do to manage your time is to plan. You can't ever manage time, but you can manage what you do with the time you have.

Here's how to leverage the time you have to live the life you want:

1. Write a list of the things that are important to you.
2. Write down the things you are doing instead of doing the things that you just wrote that are important to you.
3. Start doing the things that are important to you and your goals.

It's really that easy.

To find out what's important to you, look at your priorities. A friend, Eric, was transitioning frcm the corporate world to becoming an entrepreneur. He is a man of faith, so he hired a Christian Life Coach. The coach asked him what his most important things were. My friend answered:

1. God
2. Family
3. Health
4. Finances

The coach then asked Eric to write down on an Excel spreadsheet what he did the most during every half-hour of the week. As the week went on, my friend wrote down whatever he did most of in every half hour. He then emailed it to his coach and they set a date for their next session.

At their next session, the coach shocked Eric. "Why did you lie to me?'

Eric was confused and a little upset. "What do you mean? I didn't lie to you. Why would I hire you to coach me if I was going to lie to you? I wrote down everything I did for the bulk of every half hour like you asked."

The coach backed off a little. "I believe you wrote what you did every half hour. That's not what I'm talking about. You lied to me when you said the most important things in your life are God, your family, your health, and your finances. By seeing how you spend your time, your television is the most important thing to you. Where is your one-on-one time with God? You work from home now; where is the dedicated time to your kids when they come home from school?"

Eric says that the shock of the truth humbled him. He had thought he was living up to his morals and values. He looked again at the week he had lived and didn't see his priorities listed there. He was speechless.

"This is what I'd like to do," the coach said. "Let's use the same spreadsheet style and write down the life you think you've been living. Let's write out our perfect week."

Eric started with when he woke up. He wrote: *Coffee with Jesus.* He then made sure to add to his calendar and block out time for the things he said were his priorities. That exercise changed Eric's life for the better. Today, he lives a purposeful life. Whenever he feels like he's not using his time wisely, he writes how he is going to live the next week and gets back to living up to his priorities. He says, "When I write down what I'm going to do in the upcoming week, it's me telling time what to do. I manage time, it doesn't manage me."

My calendar is essential. I would miss 75% of what I'm supposed to do if I didn't use one. If something gets on my calendar, it gets done. It doesn't matter if I like it or not, it gets done. My mood doesn't dictate what I do; it's too unstable.

I don't look forward to getting up earlier than I'm accustomed to, getting in the car when it's still dark and cold outside, or getting to the gym and working out. Then, when my long workday is finished at around 8 PM, the last thing I want to do is continue writing this book. But it's on my calendar. I put it there with intentionality based on my priorities and goals. I trust this book will bless you, which would mean I used the time to write it wisely.

Find an accountability partner. Share your goals and aspirations with them and then allow them to keep you accountable if you start slacking. Give them the freedom to call you on your laziness. They're not yelling at you; they're helping you fight your bad habits.

Sadly, not enough people know how to take constructive feedback. It takes humility and courage to allow someone to call you out on your foolishness. At writer's groups, the person whose work is critiqued cannot talk. They can't explain why they wrote what they wrote. They understand that if someone isn't clear with their writing, they should write it differently. You will not grow from great feedback if you justify your actions. Trust that the people are telling you things you may not like, but they come from a position of love. They're trying to build you up, not destroy you.

WORK-LIFE BALANCE

There needs to be more awareness of the trendy term, "work-life balance". When people think about balance, they think 50/50. So, naturally, when they hear "work-life balance," they think the same amount of energy and time that is to be spent at work is the same amount of energy and time that is to be spent at home. It adds up if you do the math. However, that math doesn't add up in the real world.

If you are driven to succeed at something great, you must devote more time to it than anything else. Sometimes, the work-life balance is 80/20. This might look harsh, but if you find the perfect partner who shares your goals and dreams and pushes you to get them, they'll be okay. They know that the 20% spent with them will be with 100% of your attention.

They also know that you'll be on vacation soon, and it will be 10/90—with 90% of the time devoted to them. Great teams/couples talk like this:

"I'll make it up to you."

"Thanks for allowing me to put that overtime in. This weekend, we'll do whatever you want."

"I can't wait to buy you that purse you told me about two months ago."

"Let's take your parents out to a nice dinner."

Work-life balance is not a one-size-fits-all shoe. Find the balance that works in your home and you'll live a happy life.

CHAPTER 11
PROCRASTINATION

DREAM KILLER

When people think of dream killers, they think of haters, drugs, alcohol, deception, and things of that nature. However, I propose that procrastination is the biggest killer of goals and dreams. Everyone knows how to eat healthy. Everyone knows they should exercise. Everyone knows they should read books. Why don't they? Because they procrastinate! They wait and wait and wait and then they start with their excuses:

I'll start on Monday.

I have to do this other thing first.

Enter your excuse here:

Procrastination is a monster. However, it's not unbeatable. The best weapon to defeat procrastination is knowing your passion and purpose—knowing your WHY. My why drives me to walk right past procrastination without looking back. My why fuels me, not my excuses. My previous success gives me confidence that the future success I'm shooting for will be mine. Read these next two sentences twice—You've already procrastinated enough. Make that move already!

8 WAYS TO BEAT PROCRASTINATION

1. <u>Set Clear Goals.</u> Clearly define what you want to achieve and break down your goals into smaller, manageable tasks. This will make your action items less overwhelming.
2. <u>Create a Schedule.</u> Develop a schedule or a to-do list outlining specific tasks and deadlines. Then, put them in your calendar and promise to yourself that whatever makes it in your calendar is important enough to take priority over anything else at that designated moment. Prioritize your tasks based on importance, urgency, and as they relate to your goals. Stick to your calendar as much as possible. This will create consistency that will create momentum that will create wins.
3. <u>Eliminate Distractions.</u> Identify and remove distractions that prevent you from staying focused on your tasks. Turn off the notifications from your phone. Find a quiet place to work. Set a time limit on your phone for the apps that suck up too much of your time. Lock the door. Talk to family members beforehand and let them know you are not to be bothered unless the house is on fire.
4. <u>Use Time Management Techniques.</u> Don't work yourself to the bone all at once. Just as going to the gym for the first time and working out way too hard is going to make you sore and you won't go again, overworking does the same to your mind and it will try to stop you from doing it again. Use techniques such as the Pomodoro Technique—work for a set amount of time followed by a short break (or short breaks).
5. <u>Break Tasks into Smaller Steps.</u> One of the biggest reasons for procrastination is when we feel overwhelmed. If a task seems daunting and you see yourself shying away from doing it, break it down into

smaller, more manageable steps If you're an entrepreneur, hire someone else to do the things you need for your business that you hate to do. Hire a Virtual Assistant on an as-needed basis and have him or her do the things you don't like to do, allowing you to do the things you love to do for the business.

6. Reward Yourself. Gift yourself rewards for completing tasks or reaching milestones. This will keep you motivated and a motivated you is a dangerous you! Provide yourself with positive reinforcements along the journey to success.

7. Give Yourself Grace. Practice self-compassion and understand that everyone procrastinates from time to time. Don't give up just because you didn't do much yesterday. Today is a new day. Be kind to yourself and move forward. Don't dwell on time misspent and manage the time at hand.

8. Seek Support. If you're struggling to overcome procrastination on your own, consider an accountability partner or hiring a coach. Seek help from friends, family, a therapist, a pastor, or a coach. You're not alone. God has put provision in your path in the forms of people who are willing to provide encouragement, accountability, and additional strategies for overcoming procrastination.

Beating procrastination takes effort and dedicated time. Trust me, it's worth the effort and time to give a better effort on your goals and to enjoy more quality time.

CHAPTER 12

DEVELOPING EMOTIONAL INTELLIGENCE FOR SUCCESS AND RELATIONSHIPS

EQ

The term, Emotional Intelligence, was birthed by two researchers, Peter Salavoy and John Mayer, in their article "Emotional Intelligence" in the journal Imagination, Cognition, and Personality in 1990. Author Dan Goleman popularized it in his 1995 book *Emotional Intelligence*.

I thought long and hard about adding this topic because I believe so many people have misused the term and that readers might assume they know what this chapter is about, albeit based on faulty information. In the end, knowing about and mastering emotional intelligence, although having many facets, is much too important of a topic not to shed light on, especially as it relates to living a successful life.

The definition has gone through various meanings, but the stabilized definition of Emotional Intelligence—also referred to as EQ—is this: *The ability to understand, use, and manage your own emotions in positive ways to relieve stress, communicate effectively, empathize with others, overcome challenges, and defuse conflict.*

As you can see, when you put these words together and form emotional intelligence, it has to do with managing yourself, relieving stress in your life, having excellent communication skills, realizing what's going on with others around you, the talent to overcome challenges, and to defuse conflict once it starts or to defuse it before it can even begin. That's a lot, but emotional intelligence is even more still.

It is the ability to respond or react in any given situation without losing or sacrificing your character and integrity. Emotionally intelligent people respond and react with reason and thoughtfulness, not emotion.

At the time of this writing, this country is going on eight years of a vicious political divide. We are living through perhaps the most significant political disagreements since the Vietnam War and the Civil War. The two most significant political systems in this country, along with the news media, interference from other countries, and the world of social media where things are recorded and viewed in real-time, with no explanation of context —have literally torn this country in half. You have very intelligent people with PhDs, doctorates, scientists, successful entrepreneurs, and those in law enforcement on both sides. You have Christians on one side and Christians on the other side, as well as atheists on each side. We live in an age when, around the dinner table, it is parents against their children or brother against brother.

The presidential election sparks arguments on the streets or social media. When some people realize that their "friend" believes in the opposing party's politics, they argue for the world to see before they "unfriend" them for life.

What, you may ask, does the political landscape have to do with my journey to success and emotional intelligence? I'm glad you asked.

Grab your scuba gear for the rest of this chapter; I'm about to take you to deep waters.

Let's say you're a registered Democrat sitting next to a person wearing a MAGA hat, how do you react? How do you react? I've seen people demand that person take the hat off. I've seen students want other students kicked out of the school or class-room. That, dear reader, is not having emotional intelligence.

A person with emotional intelligence will respond in one of two ways:

1. They wouldn't even mention politics. This is how you defuse an argument before it has the chance to start.
2. They would engage in a civil conversation based on facts, not bias.

The person lacking EQ will make faces, look annoyed, start an argument, ask to be moved, or create an atmosphere that could escalate to violence.

Good leaders and good partners have a good grasp of EQ. They have the ability to read the room. A good husband should know his wife is mad at him after three seconds of being in the same room. A good leader should know that Sheila is not having a good day because she didn't give him her usual smile and fist-bump.

Emotionally Intelligent people know how to read the room. Bad leaders go into rooms to impose their superiority, while good leaders make sure everyone is okay so they would be more recep-tive to the coming changes. Good leaders know it's better to post-pone a meeting so that someone in the meeting has time to cool down. Bad leaders rush two hotheads into a room to "talk it out" and are surprised when foul language, accusations, and secrets get blurted out in anger, and maybe some furniture moving takes place.

For the leaders or managers responsible for an organization's production, the most powerful tool you wield is not your title nor the authority to fire people. It's EQ, understanding the people who work for you and empathizing with their emotions. Mind you, you don't have to validate the feelings of someone who is not being logical, but you must be empathetic to it.

THE POWER OF PERSPECTIVE

Understanding that not being culturally myopic—that my way is the only way—is the way to do anything extraordinary. Social sensitivity is now a fabric of our society, whether you like it or not. We are a few short years away from going through the only global pandemic we've seen in our lifetimes. COVID-19 has changed the world as we knew it.

Millions of people, close friends, and beloved family members died unexpectedly. Bodies were left in apartment building hallways for weeks in New York City. People's livelihoods were taken from them. Millions of people doing well financially before the pandemic were forced to declare bankruptcy. Every big and small company had to figure out how to keep some sort of production going when no one was supposed to go outside. After all, people kept eating; lights were still being used, and people needed their faith more than ever but couldn't go to church. Leaders with EQ found ways to motivate and retain their employees. Leaders with no EQ found that their workforce had diminished tremendously as people had the time to reflect on their working conditions.

After the pandemic, the workplace around the world changed. Generational perspectives suddenly became visible regarding whether someone would rather work at the office, at their home, at a coffee shop, or a hybrid of all three. Leaders had to deal with Baby Boomers, Gen X, Millennials, and Gen Z, who all voiced their opinions on how to reshape the workplace once the world opened up again. I'm not giving a history lesson of what you've lived through. I'm laying this out to tell you that the companies that survived weren't always those with the best service or products. It was those companies that were led by emotionally intelligent leaders.

HOW I BRIDGED THE DIVIDE ON MY JOURNEY TO SUCCESS

My road to success put me in the position of working with people I would not have preferred to hang out with because of our differences. I am a very proud black man. I would be hard to miss if I entered a room, being that I'm over six feet tall. I very much support the politics I vote for, not out of cultural preference, but because of study and the actions I've seen take place or not take place in minority communities. That being said, as I was working my way up, and to this day, I have had to work extensively with individuals with opposing political views.

People with high EQ continue to keep the main thing the main thing; they're able to not lose sight of their goals. I didn't have the luxury of picking the people in a position to help me.

> "I HAD TO FIND A WAY TO WORK WITH WHOMEVER GOD PUT IN MY PATH."

I had to find a way to work with whomever God put in my path. Thankfully, people on the other side of the political spectrum also have a grasp of emotional intelligence. We could see the benefits of a business relationship, and even though some other things weren't aligned, our business goals were aligned to the point that they trumped our political views.

We were able to utilize our strengths and resources. We wouldn't talk about politics or whatever rhetoric of the week came from the far left or far right. We would focus on the positive things we needed to accomplish, whose task it was to oversee and accomplish what, what were the metrics to ensure we were tracking in the right direction, what course of action we would take if we had to reassess and improve, and every other thing a good company does to serve its clients to the best of their ability.

I've worked very well with many Republicans. In fact, I call them great business partners and even friends. There was a white male baby boomer Republican, a white male Gen X Republican, and another white male Republican about my age. We respectfully discussed deliverables, the best way to train our staff, how we would become the company we wanted to be, and how not just to meet compliance standards but go above and beyond what was expected of us. Our mission was not who ran the country or the politics of the day; it was having a solid business that gave back to the community and delivered a great ROI.

I have been in business with them for more than ten years. As I mentioned, we consider ourselves friends. During the last few years, some tragic events unfolding on the front page of every newspaper, social media home page, and news channel—white police officers had murdered black males. Tempers ran red-hot. Anger and rage spilled onto the streets of many cities in the form of riots and looting. Then, George Floyd got murdered on video. Racial tensions exploded!

The Black Lives Matter movement was at a fever pitch. Chaos was wafting through every major city and many towns. Yet, during this time, my white colleagues called me. They wanted to know if, in any way, they had failed me. "Have we done anything to make you feel uncomfortable or disrespected?" It made me feel very good that they would dare open that conversation with me. There were some things I could have said, but nothing of note. So, both parties utilized a high level of EQ, and our company continued to get stronger and more successful.

My most pivotal and successful relationships in business and as a professional came at the hands of white men and women. I thank God for giving me favor with them. Some might say my success came at the hands of white people because there aren't enough blacks in those positions. While that may be true, it doesn't change the fact, and nor will I not learn the lessons God had me go through, that those individuals helped me to transition from where I was to where I am. I'll also say this: I've since encountered black men that I thought would have been great for my career, only for them not to extend an olive branch. I'm writing this book, in part, for the black and brown community to do what they didn't do for me.

At the time of this writing, I am going through the process of being indoctrinated into the Tampa Bay Business Hall of Fame. It's a great honor and I'm humbled by it. Out of the 150 people who made it, only six blacks are among them. I firmly believe that my business EQ helped me get to this position. A black businesswoman nominated me, yet a white woman is the one pushing for my indoctrination.

What I would say to my younger, eager-to-succeed black and brown men and women in business is to keep your professional life professional if you want to succeed. Don't be headstrong and think you can't align with someone vastly different from how you look and think. If you're too stuck on ideologies and rhetoric, you'll limit your success. However, if you utilize the people God puts in your path, you'll see that whatever your thoughts of color and discrimination will turn upside down. God will use people you wouldn't expect to do the unexpected in ways that will catapult you to another hemisphere.

THE LEARNING CURVE TO TRIUMPHS

Knowing that you don't understand everything yet is a beautiful piece of wisdom to operate by. Those who know everything can't learn anything. As a business owner and father, I've discovered that for the best of things, the things of most value, there is usually a time of preparation and learning. It's not easy to do, but once you realize the time and effort it will take to learn something, you'll not be so upset and down on yourself when you experience setbacks. Happier people use their Emotional Intelligence to guard their moods from tanking when they've tripped up.

There's no road map to being a good parent. There's also no roadmap for being a great spouse, leader, entrepreneur, church leader, community leader, etc. Sure, there are guidelines to operate from within, but no one has handed me a step-by-step instructional manual on doing those things. There's no one way to do those things either. There's no one-size-fits-all Dorothy shoe to take you from where you are to Kansas. Embrace the learning curve because once you figure out one thing, you're going to have to figure out what to do next. The learning curve is perpetual.

Short-cutting things of importance sows the seeds for long-standing misery, regardless of any instant satisfaction you may get. When you try to go too fast or cut corners on excellence, you are closer to failure than success because you break the Law of Sacrifice.

CHAPTER 13
THE CRUCIBLE OF LEADERSHIP

BETRAYAL

I now want to delve into a topic that is rarely discussed, but yet incredibly pivotal in a person's growth—the transformative power of betrayal. Let's examine how such experiences, though painful, can cultivate resilience, wisdom, and a deeper under-standing of human nature—qualities essential for effective leadership.

Betrayal, a word that evokes feelings of hurt, anger, and confu-sion, is often seen as a negative experience. However, in the paradoxical journey of leadership, betrayal can serve as a critical and evolutionary experience. While it is a pain-inducing teacher, its lessons are invaluable, cultivating resilience, empathy, and strategic foresight in leaders.

Through historical and contemporary examples, let's explore how betrayal shapes leaders, using the story of Judas's betrayal of Christ, the political maneuvering of Julius Caesar, the complexities of leadership faced by Martin Luther King Jr, and the corporate intrigue faced by Elizabeth Holmes.

THE DIVINE BETRAYAL: LEARNING FORGIVENESS AND RESILIENCE

The story of Judas Iscariot's betrayal of Jesus Christ stands as one of the most poignant examples of treachery. Judas, one of the twelve apostles, led soldiers to Jesus in exchange for thirty pieces of silver. This act led to Christ's crucifixion! It was an event of profound betrayal, yet central to Christian redemption narratives.

This ultimate act of treachery was pivotal for the fulfillment of Christ's mission and teachings. For leaders, this story underscores the power of forgiveness and resilience. Christ's response to betrayal, focusing on forgiveness and fulfilling his mission, exemplifies how leaders can confront betrayal not with vengeance but with a steadfast commitment to their principles and goals. It teaches leaders that betrayal, while painful, can strengthen resolve and clarify purpose.

A logical response to this exposition about Jesus's response might be, "I'm not Jesus." Yes, I get it, nor am I suggesting that any of us possess the capacity to always respond with unselfishness, grace, and untainted love. We do, however, control *how* we respond.

There is a common need to make ourselves into victims. I have been there. This victim mindset causes us to see other's behaviors, certainly when it hurts us, as purely malicious and unwarranted. But, dear reader, if we shift our perspective to one of curiosity and begin to question how we can grow from every experience, no matter the degree of betrayal, maybe, just maybe, we can see a greater significance. Leaders keep their eyes focused on the bigger picture.

KNOW THIS...

Even the people who betray you are part of the plan.

The Messiah couldn't fulfill His mission if it weren't for Judas.

THE POLITICAL CHESSBOARD: JULIUS CAESAR AND THE ULTIMATE BETRAYAL

The assassination of Julius Caesar stands as one of history's most iconic betrayals, immortalized by Shakespeare's famous line, "Et tu, Brute?"—*You, too, Brutus?* This act of treachery was not merely personal but a seismic event that altered the course of Roman history. Caesar, a military general and statesman, was betrayed by those he considered allies and friends, including Brutus, whom he trusted deeply.

This story serves as a stark reminder to leaders about the volatile nature of power and the complexities of human relationships. Caesar's betrayal underscores the importance of political acumen and the necessity for leaders to be vigilant and discerning, particularly in environments where allegiances can shift rapidly. The event teaches that trust should be extended judiciously and that understanding the motivations and ambitions of those around you is crucial for survival and success in any leadership role.

Furthermore, Caesar's assassination demonstrates the double-edged sword of leadership ambition. While his quest for power enabled him to accomplish great things for Rome, it also isolated him and made him a target. Leaders must, therefore, balance ambition with humility and awareness, ensuring that they do not become blind to the dynamics and potential threats within their own circles.

Just as you're not Jesus, you're not Caesar either, obviously, but there are several lessons that you can take from Caesar's demise and add to your leadership toolkit. Among them is to balance ambition and caution. Caesar's ambition led him to accumulate unprecedented power, which alarmed many who feared the end of the Republic and the rise of a dictator.

As a leader, balance your own ambition with caution, considering the broader implications of your actions. Likewise, pay attention to the ambition levels of those around, tread with caution around those whose ambition is not constrained by healthy doses of humility, empathy, and restraint.

KNOW THIS…

In the chambers where loyalty should have thrived, daggers of deceit delivered the final blow, reminding us that even the greatest can fall when treachery is veiled in friendship.

THE COMPLEXITIES OF LEADERSHIP: MARTIN LUTHER KING JR.

The civil rights movement in the United States provides a poignant backdrop for understanding betrayal within leadership. Martin Luther King Jr., a paragon of nonviolent resistance, experienced betrayal not from enemies but within his inner circle and from fellow black leaders. Figures like Adam Clayton Powell Jr. threatened to expose King's personal vulnerabilities to undermine his leadership, while others criticized his strategies and distanced themselves to advance their agendas.

These betrayals, rather than crippling King, honed his leadership. They taught him to navigate the complex dynamics of human relationships and politics, reinforcing the necessity of staying true to one's principles amidst internal dissent and external pressures. King's ability to maintain focus on the larger vision of racial equality, despite betrayals, demonstrates how leaders can transform personal attacks into strengths, fostering resilience and a more profound commitment to their cause.

KNOW THIS…

As you become wiser as a leader you realize that your diet isn't just what you eat, it's what you watch, what you read, who you follow and who you spend your time with. So if your goal is to be a transforma-tional leader, you have to start by removing the junk from your diet.

THE TRUST BETRAYAL: ELIZABETH HOLMES

In the modern corporate world, the story of Elizabeth Holmes exemplifies a different kind of betrayal—that of public and investor trust. Holmes, the founder of Theranos, promised to revolutionize healthcare with technology that could conduct comprehensive tests using just a few drops of blood. However, the technology was fraudulent, and her deceit not only led to the downfall of her company but also endangered the health of individuals who relied on her tests.

Holmes's story is a cautionary tale for leaders about the ethical responsibilities that come with their positions. It demonstrates the catastrophic consequences of betraying the trust of stakeholders and the public. Leaders are reminded that integrity and honesty are the cornerstones of sustainable success. Betraying trust for personal gain or out of hubris can lead to irreversible damage, not only to one's career but also to the lives of others and to the fabric of society.

This case also illustrates the importance of transparency and accountability in leadership. By fostering an environment where truth is valued and ethical behavior is non-negotiable, leaders can avoid the pitfalls of deceit and ensure the long-term health and success of their organizations.

KNOW THIS…

Honesty and integrity are absolutely essential for success in life—all areas of life. The really good news is that anyone can develop both honesty and integrity." —Zig Ziglar

LEADERS AND LOYALTY

Leaders highly value loyalty, particularly in the wake of betrayal, for several crucial reasons that underscore the fabric of successful leadership and organizational cohesion.

Firstly, loyalty in the face of betrayal acts as a stabilizing force, maintaining the integrity and morale of a team or community. When a leader faces betrayal, it can create a climate of suspicion and fear, undermining the collective trust that binds the group.

However, the presence of loyal individuals provides a counter-balance to this disruption. These loyal members reinforce the leader's vision and authority, helping to mitigate the fallout of betrayal and maintain continuity in the group's purpose and direction. For a leader, such loyalty becomes invaluable, serving as a testament to their leadership's worth and as a rallying point for reestablishing unity and focus.

Secondly, loyalty following a betrayal serves as a litmus test for the leader's influence and the authenticity of their relationships. True loyalty is revealed not in times of prosperity, but in moments of crisis. Leaders value this loyalty as it not only affirms their leadership qualities but also identifies those individuals who are genuinely committed to the cause and principles of the organization. This understanding enables leaders to build a more committed and aligned inner circle, enhancing their strategic decision-making, and reinforcing the resilience of their leadership against future challenges.

Lastly, loyalty in such times acts as a source of personal and professional growth for leaders. Betrayal, while painful, provides leaders with unique insights into human behavior, trust dynamics, and their leadership approach. Loyal followers offer support and feedback, enabling leaders to reflect, learn, and adapt.

This growth fosters a more empathetic, wise, and effective leadership style. Therefore, loyalty, especially in the aftermath of betrayal, is not just a pillar of support but also a catalyst for transformation, enabling leaders to emerge from the ordeal stronger, more enlightened, and more capable of guiding their followers toward shared goals.

THE SILVER LINING OF BETRAYAL

Betrayal, while one of the most challenging experiences a leader can face, is also one of the most instructive. The stories I've shared show that while betrayal can be a source of great pain, it can also serve as a crucial turning point, offering opportunities for reflection, learning, and growth.

Leadership, forged in the crucible of betrayal, emerges stronger, more empathetic, and more resilient. These stories remind us that the true measure of a leader is not their capacity to avoid betrayal but their ability to navigate its treacherous waters, to forgive, learn, and ultimately, to emerge more dedicated and effective than before.

In the end, betrayal, though a bitter pill, is a teacher like no other. It is an invitation to reaffirm one's values, to reassess and strengthen one's vision, and to demonstrate grace under fire. For those aspiring to lead, embracing this uncomfortable truth is not an option but a necessity.

CHAPTER 14
FROM ORDINARY TO EXTRAORDINARY

THREE FEET FROM GOLD

There's a story in Napoleon Hill's book that I can never forget. This is one of the stories that push me when I'm tired, when things don't look like they're going to end well, when unexpected disasters materialize, and when I'm just plain feeling lazy.

The name of the story is Three Feet From Gold. It's a lengthy narrative, so I'll paraphrase it for you:

A young man goes west to dig for gold. After weeks, he finds gold! He covers up the mine, returns to his family, and convinces them to help him buy drilling equipment. He comes back to the mine with the necessary machinery, and soon enough, they start digging up gold!

However, soon after, the vein of gold disappeared. They had come to the end of the rainbow but the pot of gold was no longer there. They desperately tried to find the gold again but to no avail.

Finally, they decided to QUIT.

He sold the machinery for a few hundred dollars to a "Junk Man." That same junk man gets expert advice and starts drilling again. He found more gold than he ever imagined possible.

The gold was just three feet from where the others had stopped drilling!

The story continues to say that the man who quit—R. U. Darby—later became wealthy from selling insurance. "I stopped three feet from gold, but I will never stop because men say 'no' when I ask them to buy insurance."

I share this story with you because you will experience frustrations and failures on your Journey to Success. Don't quit. Whatever you do, if you have a passion for something, if you're doing something that is attached to your purpose and your 'why,' don't ever quit.

 "One of the most common causes of failure is the habit of quitting when overtaken by temporary defeat."

NAPOLEON HILL, *THINK AND GROW RICH*

There is no way to escape the trap that is ordinary and become extraordinary if you quit. You don't have to be a superhuman not to quit. You are surrounded by people that have not quit. They may not have reached their ultimate goals, but they're still in the fight. As long as they don't quit, they'll never lose.

TYLER PERRY

Tyler Perry was born Emmitt Perry Jr. in New Orleans, Louisiana, on September 14, 1969. He was born to a loving mother but an incredibly abusive father, Emmitt Perry, who he was named after. His mother, his two sisters, and he endured countless beatings and berating's from Emmitt. It got so bad that his mother packed them in a car, and they escaped to California. However, his father reported the car stolen and was able to find them. Tyler recounts how his father beat his mother the entire way back home.

After a particularly intense beating by his father with the cord of a vacuum cleaner that left welts all over his body, young Perry had enough. He legally changed his name to Tyler, not wanting to share a name with his father. He was rarely in his house, which caused him to be vulnerable in the streets. Men and women abused him during his early teens. Tyler was confused, angry, and isolated in a world of pain. No one would have thought that this broken boy would become the success he is today.

In a 1991 Oprah Winfrey show, she said writing down your life events could be healing. Tyler decided to find out. He began to write in a journal every day after watching that episode. Those writings became the foundation of his first play, *I know I've Been Changed*.

After battling through emotions of fear and inadequacy, he went all in on making his play a colossal hit and becoming a star. He spent his entire savings—$12,000—to produce and promote it. Only thirty people attended it, and most of them were family members of the cast.

Broke and penniless, he was forced to sleep in homeless shelters. He slept in his car for three straight months, unable to get back on his feet. His mother urged him to get a real job but Tyler was convinced that the world would love his plays. "One day, I'll entertain millions with my stories."

By 2024, his films and shows have grossed over $660 million, and his net worth is estimated at $1 billion. He owns his own movie studio, and in 2008, he purchased the Fort McPherson U.S. Army base where most of his movies are filmed.

When I see Tyler Perry, whether he is dressed as Madea or preaching in front of thousands of people, I am reminded of the hell he went through. I am proud of the man he is today, but prouder of his teenage self, because he didn't quit. He could have been a bad statistic, a criminal, an abuser, or worse. But he didn't let his upbringing or his first play's failure define him.

Mostly, I'm humbled by his forgiving heart. When he found out Emmitt was not his biological father, he saw him in a different light. Tyler provides for the sprawling home in which Emmitt lives. Their relationship has taken a turn, to the point that they laugh about Tyler's early years. During an interview, Tyler was asked how he was able to accomplish all he did. Tyler said it was because of the adversity he went through as a kid. It showed him that nothing could break him.

After that interview, Emmitt famously joked via a text to Tyler: *If I had beat your ass one more time, you could have been the President of the United States!*

TOM BRADY

Thomas Edward Patrick Brady Jr. was born on August 3, 1977, in San Mateo, California. He was the youngest of four and the only boy. The story of his poor showing at the NFL combine has become legendary, especially his slow 40-yard dash, if you could call it a dash. He was drafted in the 6th of 7 rounds of the NFL draft by the New England Patriots. The confusing part wasn't that they had drafted him so late; it was more that they already had enough quarterbacks.

Patriots coach Bill Belichick would later say he knew Brady was a leader by how he interacted with the other rookies. These other rookies had been drafted ahead of Brady, but somehow, he led them. The following year, the Patriots released two quarterbacks because of the work Brady was putting in on the practice field and the respect he was getting from his teammates.

Starting quarterback Drew Bledsoe got hurt, and Brady stepped in. He led the Patriots to a surprising 11-5 finish. Brady had solidified his spot as the starter. He would win more Super Bowls than any player in NFL history, with seven.

I share Brady's story with you, ever though I'm not a Tom Brady fan, per se. However, I am impressed with his leadership and the work he must have done when no one was looking. In your journey from going to extraordinary from ordinary, know that you'll have to put in work while no one notices.

Don't worry about accolades, put in the work.

Don't worry about trophies, put in the work.

Don't worry about the number of zeros you want in your bank account, put in the work.

Don't worry about getting tripped up, get up and put in the work.

If you put in the work and don't quit, you are already extraordinary; it will just take time for everyone to see it.

OPRAH WINFREY

As a child, Oprah Winfrey wore potato sacks because her poverty-stricken family rarely had the budget for clothes. Let that sentence sink in…

Oprah was sent to live with her grandmother because her unwed teenage mother couldn't find work. When her grand-mother died, she went to live in a boarding house in Milwaukee. Not only did she experience extreme poverty, but she also endured years of sexual and physical abuse—raped for the first time at 9 years old by her 19-year-old cousin.

She forced herself out of that situation and moved in with her father at 14 in Nashville, Tennessee. Her dad provided protection, direction, discipline, and a sense of structure. By her senior year, she had secured a full scholarship to Tennessee State University. However, she left college early to pursue a career in media at 19.

She became the first black female news anchor before the age of 20 before landing a co-anchor spot in Baltimore. She was sexually harassed and occasionally humiliated at her job but she didn't quit. She wouldn't need to. She was fired seven months after she joined.

She didn't stay down for long and landed a job hosting the then-stagnant morning talk show, "AM Chicago." In a few short months, Oprah turned it from the lowest-rated talk show in Chicago to the highest-rated. Three years later, the show was renamed "The Oprah Winfrey Show."

In 1986, she founded Harpo Productions, her own production company. She then negotiated ownership of "The Oprah Winfrey Show," which, at its peak, brought in $300 million a year. She now also owns a magazine, a radio channel, and has partnered with Discovery Communications to launch her cable channel, the Oprah Winfrey Network.

Being abused is, sadly, not all that uncommon. The difference between Oprah and others who have been molested is that she did not let those moments define her. She did not want people to think of her as a victim. She wanted people to see an intelligent, quick-witted, black female pioneering her career predominantly held by Caucasians. To become extraordinary, you can't allow past failures, regrets, and even beatings and rapes from creating a brighter future for you.

DAYMOND JOHN

Daymond John's father walked out of his life and never looked back when he was 10. His mother raised him in the lower middle-class area of New York City, Hollis Queens. He learned the value of hard work early, beginning with his first apprenticeship to an electrician when he was 10. Then, a sound, a movement, a phenomenal beat and rhythm birthed in the Bronx made its way into Queens called Hip Hop.

Daymond was obsessed with it to the point that he wanted to be part of it. However, he lacked the lyrical brilliance many others had, such as Run DMC and LL Cool J. As Hip Hop started to take over the country, one company called Timberland didn't like that they were wearing their boots. There is new ownership now, but the owner at the time famously said, "We don't sell our boots to drug dealers." Daymond, a hard-working waiter at Red Lobster, not a drug dealer, got very upset. Then, other famous brands started saying they didn't want the Hip Hop culture to wear their brands either.

Daymond talked to three of his friends, and they started a clothing company called FUBU—For Us By Us. Well, it was more of an idea at that point. Daymond clarified, "FUBU is not about color, it's about a culture."

They took out ads in publications such as Right On magazine. The first people to buy their clothing were teenage kids in Seattle and Hip Hop fans in Japan. FUBU was on to something. They expected to sell in and around New York City but had already gone national and global. For two years, they would go to video shoots with the same ten shirts and beg artists to wear them in their MTV videos at least for a few seconds. They would take the same ten shirts and offer them to another artist and another and another.

LL Cool J, also from Hollis, said, "We're going to pay it forward. We need to support people in the neighborhood." He agreed to wear FUBU as much as he could. He wore a black FUBU hat in a GAP commercial. LL Cool J dropped the phrase "For Us By Us" in that commercial—FUBU had arrived.

However, they still only had very limited clothes. Daymond took a loan out at his house and spent $100,000 converting his home into a mini factory. However, they had a problem, they had many more orders than they could fulfill at the makeshift factory. Daymond's mother took out a loan and put an ad in the New York Times— "Millions of Dollars in Orders. Need Financing."

Loan sharks came from the north, south, east, and west. However, Daymond struck a distribution deal with Bruce and Norman Weisfeld. FUBU became a global brand and brought in millions of dollars a year. Then, Daymond got cast for Shark Tank. The genius behind FUBU was no longer a hidden figure. He then got asked to be a part of President Obama's "My Brother's Keeper" initiative, along with John Legend, Alonzo Mourning, and Shaquille O'Neal.

Today, Daymond John, businessman, fashion designer, author, and television personality, has a net worth of $350 million.

What draws my interest in Daymond's story is that he was willing to go all in. He gave everything he had to turn his house into a factory. He traveled on fumes to get to video shoots and didn't let his ego stop him from practically begging people to wear his clothes. To go from ordinary to extraordinary, you must be willing to give it everything you've got. Everyone wants to be great, but only some are willing to give all they have to attain it.

There are many more stories of people who have come from nothing and done something exceptional.

- Sarah Blakely—went from department store to department store, sneaking in and selling her Spanx. She is the first female entrepreneur billionaire.
- Serena Williams came from a gang-riddled, crime-infested part of Los Angeles to dominate the game of tennis.
- Shahid Kahn—immigrated to the US from Pakistan. He washed dishes while attending university, making $1.20 an hour. His current net worth is $7.9 billion.
- Roman Abramovich—He lost both of his parents when he was three years old. He was raised by relatives, jumping from house to house. He worked as a street trader as well as a mechanic at a factory before finding significant success. His net worth is estimated at $14.4 billion.
- Larry Ellison—the founder of Oracle. He was born to an unwed mother who gave him up for adoption when he contracted pneumonia at 9 months old. His adoptive father had lost a fortune in the Great Depression. His adoptive mother then passed away. Larry bounced from job to job until he created Oracle and is easily now one of the wealthiest people in the world. His net worth is a staggering $88.4 billion.

There are other stories of success your pastors, your friend's parents, judges, pilots, restaurant owners, etc. Success is all around you and it doesn't always have to be about money.

HOW TO BECOME EXTRAORDINARY

You need to have a lot of things going for you to become extraordinary. However, if I were to strip it down to the two basic necessities, here they are:

1. **A divine purpose**. This will pull you to action no matter how comfortable you get. It's an inner drive that fear and laziness can't reach. For me, I knew I wasn't meant to get up early and work for someone else. I couldn't rest until I started my own business. My purpose drove me to study, research, and act.

2. **A healthy competitive spirit**. You don't get like Brady, Serena, Oprah, or anyone great without a healthy competitive spirit. A strong desire to win is not about ego, it's about purpose. I never hate on people who have achieved a high level of success. On the contrary, I'm happy for them. However, part of me also starts an internal dialogue—*Wow, look at what he's accomplished. Why am I not doing something like that? This group is doing half a billion. Great for them, but if they can do it, I can, too!*

I continue to ask you to write down your purpose because, if you don't, you will not unlock the full power contained in these pages. What does an extraordinary life look like for you? Is it to be a homeowner before 30? That's what it was for me in my 20s. I worked long 13-to 15-hour days, but I achieved it. The feeling I had when I was given the keys to my very own home in my 20s was exhilarating. The ability to provide for my family at a level better than anyone ever did at that age was extremely rewarding. I loved that feeling so much I continued to push myself repeatedly to feel that feeling over and over again.

My struggle now is not giving my children so much they feel entitled. Extraordinary to me now is to have the luxury of focusing on imparting to my children the best of what I have—my relationship with God, discipline, hard work ethic, desire, tenacity, and a never-ending search for knowledge.

My legacy will not just be money and property. It has to be something of value without dollars attached to it. I want them to stand up for what they believe in, so I need to stand up for what

I believe in.

I'm beyond grateful for my daughter, Imani. She was raised with much more than what I had, yet she also has the determination and desire to do great things. At the time of this writing, Imani recently had the opportunity to be in the room and be a part of an open-heart surgery at St. Joseph's Hospital. Usually, interns are in the observation room. However, there she was, so close to the surgeon that blood squirted on her as much as the other physicians. I might have passed out. In fact, someone did get weak in the knees, but my daughter stood there, totally transfixed. Because of the social capital I have garnered, my daughter was exposed to a unique experience. This experiential learning exercise will forever change her life and catapult her toward her dream of becoming a medical doctor.

"MY LEGACY WILL NOT JUST BE MONEY AND PROPERTY."

What amazing thing will your children be able to experience because of the social capital you were able to acquire? If you want it to be extraordinary, you must start taking massive action —right now.

CHAPTER 15
THE LAW OF SACRIFICE

> If you really want to understand what it takes to be successful, don't ask, 'What does it take to get to the place that you are at?' But rather ask, 'Who and what did you have to have to give up?' Success is inextricably related to sacrifice."

> GARY T. HARTFIELD

In physics, Sir Isaac Newton invented the Three Laws of Motion. His third law states that for every action, there is an equal reaction but in the opposite direction. Simply stated, this means that when an object pushes another object, it gets pushed back in the opposite direction equally as hard. Given the facts regarding Sir Isaac Newton's third Law of Motion allows me to prove my bases for a new Law of Motion—the Law of Sacrifice.

The Law of Sacrifice states that you cannot get something you want without giving up something in return; it can be your time, a night out, certain friendships, alcohol, money, sleep, being uncomfortable, working with people you'd rather not work with, and whatever you may have to invest in getting it.

Today's society tries to deny the Law of Sacrifice at every turn, promising people they can fulfill their desires without forsaking anything. Social media ads are full of titles that promise something for nothing:

Get a 6-pack without long workouts!
Get Rich Without Having to Work Hard!
Become a Millionaire Real Estate Investor in this FREE One-Hour Webinar!
Lose Weight without giving up your Favorite Foods!
Become an Influencer by Using these Five Simple Hacks!

It's a very seductive thought, especially for the lazy, to think you can have whatever you'd like without ever paying for it. However, it's a fantasy. There is always, and always will be, a price to pay. Sure, occasionally, someone will "accidentally" get something incredible for nothing, like a rich uncle you never knew passing away and leaving you his fortune, but if you don't work for it, you'll mismanage it and lose it.

Frederick Douglas once said, "A man, at times, gets something for nothing, but it will, in his hands, amount to nothing."

Regarding leadership, world-renowned author and leadership coach John Maxwell put the Law of Sacrifice as one of his laws in his book, 21 Irrefutable Laws of Leadership. He describes it plainly: "You have to give up to go up." Meaning that you have to give compliments, give of your knowledge, give of your time, give of your patience, give of your motivation, and continually give for your team to do so well that the only way for you to go is—up!

One of the great shames of millionaires resides in the NBA society. These talented men have certainly sacrificed to get to the pinnacle of the basketball community. They have spent blood, sweat, and tears getting their bodies in great shape. They have spent countless hours in gyms or outdoor courts. So, they got what they worked so hard for, entry into the NBA.

With that NBA contract, comes millions of dollars. Sadly, most professional athletes, not just NBA players, file for bankruptcy within ten years of their playing days. Some may have had great business ideas during their playing days, but they were in strip joints instead of building teams to make those ideas manifest.

Because they didn't sacrifice humility, they were humiliated. They ended up poor because they spent no time going through the learning curve of managing wealth.

Most lottery winners suffer the same fate. Because they never sacrificed for that money, it goes almost as quickly as it got to them. What should have been a life-long turning point to wealth creation grows into poverty and even death.

The Law of Sacrifice is a divine principle. It operates beyond space and time and has no limits. In its most pure and noble form, the Law of Sacrifice is based on the Theology of Retribution, which is—you reap what you sow.

We define sacrifice as the act of giving up something highly valued for the sake of something else considered to have greater value or claim. Sacrifice does not mean giving up something for nothing. It means giving up one thing for something we believe is worth more.

Remember, anything worth having is worth sacrificing for. If you're giving up something you don't need or like, it's not a sacrifice. You can't fool the Law of Sacrifice; if you try, you'll only fool yourself.

CHAPTER 16

YOUR RELATIONSHIP WITH MONEY

MONEY

Human beings have a long history with money. It started when we saw the value in things we didn't possess or didn't have the skills to create. It began with bartering: *I'll give you these three chickens and those three female pigs for that ox.* At the time, everything was valued by what the other person was willing to trade for it.

Then, people of wealth created a system around gold and silver. It allowed wealthy people to "carry" their money and have status everywhere they went. That made a system of the Haves and Have-Nots. The poor had very little means of acquiring silver and gold. Then, the coins became cumbersome, so a paper currency was formed. Today, the world is getting away from paper money (dollar bills), and most people use digital money, such as debit cards and credit cards. We also have cryptocurrency, which is referred to as digital money or Internet money.

Regardless of the form of currency used, mankind developed an insatiable appetite for it. For many, it became their idol or another God people began to serve. This is why, in 1 Timothy 6:10, the Bible says, "For the love of money is a root of all kinds of evil. Some people, eager for money, have wandered from the faith and pierced themselves with many griefs."

This scripture has caused many people of faith to refrain from acquiring financial wealth and to condemn or criticize others who have accrued a vast amount of wealth. Since many people associate success with wealth, I found it necessary to discuss money in this book so that if you have a mental or spiritual block in acquiring money, you can overcome it.

By nature, I'm a provider first and foremost for my family, even more than a nurturer. If my family has a need for something, God has given me the ability to come up with the means of acquiring money so that I can "trade it" or "barter it" for what my family needs.

Some people will go to any lengths to provide for themselves and their families. Some people resort to illegal means to make money. We've seen it time and time again in the poor and disen-franchised communities, as well as the white-collar community.

The egregiously greedy structure of US society has promoted a cycle that causes the Have Nots to resort to extreme means when they do not have income. Frederick Douglass once said, "Where justice is denied, where poverty is enforced, where ignorance prevails, and where any one class is made to feel that society is an organized conspiracy to oppress, rob and degrade them, neither persons nor property will be safe." This quote poignantly encapsulates the desperate measures people may resort to when systematically denied the means to provide for their families.

When people lack the legal means to provide for their family and face systematic and institutional discrimination, they often resort to various coping mechanisms and alternative means of survival.

Frederick Douglass's insight underscores that such conditions— where justice is denied and poverty is enforced—can lead to a breakdown in the safety and stability of society, driving people to take desperate and often dangerous measures in the struggle for survival and dignity.

FINANCIAL LITERACY

Everyone in the world seems fixated on getting more money. But I have to share a secret with you: the Money Game is not about getting more money; it's about managing what you have. Sadly, many communities have never been taught how to manage money. In October 2020, JPMorgan Chase announced a $30 billion Racial Equity Commitment over five years to help close the racial wealth gap and advance economic inclusion in the United States. The commitment aims to provide economic opportunity to underserved communities, especially Black and Latinx communities, and includes lending, equity, and direct funding. The bank's goals for the commitment include:

- Increasing sustainable homeownership
- Expanding affordable housing
- Growing small businesses
- Supporting diverse suppliers
- Improving financial health and access to banking
- Building a more diverse and inclusive workforce

The root cause of generational poverty is that people have no idea how to manage money. They weren't taught the discipline of budgeting and living within their means for a period of time until they could ascend to a higher financial status.

To quite the contrary, marginalized people like African Americans were barred from such knowledge for hundreds of years. It would be easy to argue the role diligence and "pulling oneself up from the bootstraps" plays into this reality. I won't argue. Instead, I make these comments because they are reality.

"THE ROOT CAUSE OF GENERATIONAL POVERTY IS THAT PEOPLE HAVE NO IDEA HOW TO MANAGE MONEY."

Many people buy what they want but end up begging for what they need. Millions of intelligent, hard-working, honest people need government assistance. We live in a country where immigrants come, not speaking the language, but within two years of managing money appropriately, they start buying properties and owning businesses.

Yet, in inner-city and other disenfranchised communities, instead of buying a child a decent pair of shoes at a reasonable price, too often some of us acquiesce to their demands and buy our kids $200 Jordan's. Because we have overspent our budget, the water, electricity bill and other bills are late being paid. This causes us to accrue late fees and penalties that further exacerbate the problem. Before long, the household is caught in a relentless hamster wheel of robbing Peter to pay Paul. Finally, to avoid the utilities being cut off, we seek government assistance to rescue us from our misguided spending habits. This is the essence of "buying what we want and begging for what we need." If this is you— here comes your wakeup call. WAKE UP!

How about you don't get the $180 sneakers and get $50 sneakers (that are probably more comfortable) and put the difference in a place where it can compound in the next 20 years? Some people hear the word *compound* and instantly detach, thinking, it's too complicated. It's not! All it means is to put the money somewhere where it will grow.

When people aren't taught money management, they can't teach it to their kids. This is the crux of generational financial curses. This isn't just for those who don't have a higher level of education; this is a cultural problem, not an education problem. Many people with degrees and diplomas who don't know how to manage their money and live beyond their means also get their utilities shut off and cars repossessed. Being educated in schools doesn't make you financially literate.

A friend of mine, who has a master's degree in mathematics, relocated his family from Dallas to Orlando. He received a $14,000 relocation bonus, and after covering the moving expenses, he had about $6,000 left for additional needs. Instead of purchasing furniture, he chose to rent it from a furniture rental store. While the rented furniture looked great in his new home, he ultimately paid nearly three times its actual value by the end of the rental term. If he had bought the furniture outright, he would have saved more money and avoided a recurring bill for years on items he never owned!

Rental centers capitalize on consumers by offering an attractive, immediate solution for furnishing their homes without a large upfront cost. However, the long-term costs are significantly higher than the item's actual value, resulting in consumers paying much more over time. This approach leads to ongoing payments and financial strain, with the consumer ultimately not owning the rented items.

According to a NPR interview, "The Color of Luxury Buying," Blacks and Hispanics tend to spend nearly 30% more of their income on luxury goods compared to other demographic groups. Studies indicate that these communities allocate a larger portion of their earnings to high-status items such as designer clothing, electronics, and luxury vehicles. This spending pattern is often influenced by a variety of social and cultural factors, including the desire for social mobility, the importance of visible status symbols within their communities, and historical exclusion from certain economic opportunities. Consequently, luxury goods become a way to signal success and personal achievement, even when it requires a substantial financial commitment relative to their overall income.

CREDIT

The credit system in America began to take shape in the late 19th and early 20th centuries, with the establishment of credit bureaus and the widespread use of credit reports to evaluate an individual's creditworthiness. Initially, these systems were informal, relying on local merchants' knowledge and relationships. However, as the economy grew and consumer credit expanded, more formalized and standardized methods emerged. Unfortunately, this system was discriminatory towards Blacks and other minority groups from its inception. Redlining practices, where financial services were denied to residents of certain areas based on racial composition, and biased credit scoring algorithms, which often penalized minorities, perpetuated economic inequality. These discriminatory practices limited access to credit for Blacks and other marginalized communities, impeding their ability to purchase homes, start businesses, and build wealth, thus contributing to the enduring racial wealth gap in America. Understanding personal credit is extremely important.

Good credit puts you in play to leverage it and get better opportunities. The problem is that some people think paying their credit card debts is too expensive. That's narrow, short-term, disastrous thinking. Some people's credit scores have plummeted over a few thousand dollars. Had they paid their balances timely and accrued credit, they would have saved more than those few thousand dollars.

"**GOOD CREDIT PUTS YOU IN PLAY TO LEVERAGE IT AND GET BETTER OPPORTUNITIES.**"

For instance, if you have a credit score of 800, and I have a 600, and we both purchase the same car, your interest rate would be 2% while mine would be 10%. Consequently, your monthly payment would be $300, whereas mine would be $700. Because you were prudent with your credit, you are saving $400 each month. Another way to view this is that you're effectively making an extra $400 monthly by having a better credit score. Consider what you could do with an additional $400 a month, $4,800 a year, or $24,000 over the five-year loan term. Isn't it worth managing your credit well to achieve such significant savings?

There's a stigma out there that people with bad credit can't be trusted or in some way, lack integrity. I don't believe that. I know many people with high integrity that, for whatever reason, maybe a business failure or an illness made them late on payments. People with bad credit don't mean they never have good intentions or lack integrity Life happens. Unforeseen circumstances can strike anyone.

Tearing your Achilles while playing basketball would mean an ambulance ride, surgery, and a hospital stay. With healthcare being so convoluted and so many people not covered, that $250,000 unpaid medical bill could take them from high credit to the 400s. It can happen to anyone. Whatever your story, if you want an easier path to success, take charge of your credit score and do what you can to raise it. Trust me, this seed is worth sowing.

THE PARABLE

There is a famous parable found in Matthew 25:14-30. It states that a man went on a journey and entrusted his servants with some talents (money). To one, he gave 5; to another, he gave 2; and to the third, he gave 1. When the master returned, he inquired of each servant. The one given 5 had doubled it and gave the master back 10. The one given 2 also doubled it and gave the master back 4. However, the one who had been given 1 got scared he'd lose it. He dug it to keep it safe, and when the master returned, he gave him back the 1 talent he had been entrusted with.

The master told both the one he gave 5 and the one he gave 2, having doubled the money, "Well done, good and faithful servant. You have been faithful over a little I will set you over much. Enter into the joy of your master."

However, to the one who had been given 1 and returned only 1, he told him, "You wicked and slothful servant!" He took the 1 talent from him and gave it to the one with 10. Then, he said, "For to everyone who has will more be given, and he will have an abundance. But from the one who has not, even that will be taken away. Cast the worthless servant out, and he will experience weeping and gnashing of teeth."

Most people consider this a parable of reaping, sowing, and money. However, delightfully hidden in this story, I see a story of work ethic. The ones who had doubled the money used their energy, time, wisdom, communication skills, contacts, and work ethic. The one who buried the talent didn't even try.

If you do just enough to get by, you'll only have just enough to get by. Your perception of labor and working hard for what you want have brought you to where you are today.

If you don't like where you are today, look at the output you are giving in accordance with your talents and gifts, including the gift of time. Those willing to go above and beyond will demonstrate a better appreciation of money.

"IF YOU DON'T LIKE WHERE YOU ARE TODAY, LOOK AT THE OUTPUT YOU ARE GIVING IN ACCORDANCE WITH YOUR TALENTS AND GIFTS, INCLUDING THE GIFT OF TIME."

You don't have to be a business owner to benefit from a good work ethic. Suppose it impacts the entity you're working for. In that case, it helps the entity to do well, which maintains its ability to employ you and potentially get you bonuses or more career opportunities. If you demonstrate initiative and help the company grow, it will invest more in you.

Proverbs 22:1 says, "A good name is more desirable than great riches; to be esteemed is better than silver and gold."

As we close on this chapter about money, understand that your legacy is not only the money you leave your kids; it's also your reputation, the way people speak about you, the people you've been able to bless, and your good name. Wealth is the final representation of your character and integrity.

If you share my faith, know this—you have already inherited a kingdom. You are a prince or princess who has inherited all the riches and glory of your father. It's up to you now to have the correct mindset. With that throne comes responsibility.

"SPEAK BLESSINGS INTO EXISTENCE."

Speak blessings into existence. Say, "Father, I release all of the blessings, honor, and glory that come with being an heir to your throne." Speak it and live with the spirit of expectation. But then, work for it to happen. When it does, and it will, know how to manage it.

CHAPTER 17
GUT CHECK TIME

Dear reader, I'd like to take a moment to congratulate you on getting this far into the book. Many people buy books but, for some odd reason, don't finish them. Some people never start them. You, however, have read to near the end, and again, I want to congratulate you for wanting a better life.

However, and I am nothing if not truthful, chances are you've probably heard a similar message before, whether from other books, seminars, trainings, etc. If that's the case with you, the hard truth is that you are reading this book because **you haven't implemented the knowledge you gained** from the other books or seminars.

The knowledge of success is teeming online, on social media, in schools, in the Bible, in books, on chalkboards, and even on napkins. It's not the lack of understanding that holds people back and limits their potential; it's not acting on the knowledge that's the detriment to people reaching their goals.

It all comes down to this: If you know you aren't going to implement the steps and knowledge I spent a lifetime acquiring, which has allowed me to do very well and bless many people, bless someone you think would and gift this book to them. These words, when acted upon, contain power, and they will thank you.

However, if you have had enough of mediocrity and are ready to make a significant change in your life, give more, gain more, and live a bigger life, I can't wait for you to turn the page. Until now, I've been depositing seeds and laying the foundation for what I am going to share in the next chapter. Remember, the actions you take today can shape your future in ways you can't even imagine.

If you haven't yet, grab a Sharpie or a pen and go through the next chapter for two things:

1. To learn it.
2. To apply it.

CHAPTER 18
PUTTING IT ALL TOGETHER

GIVE BACK

A mentee recently sent me a text I'll share with you. She wrote:

> I have been observing other leaders over the past 23 hours. Why do you prefer to share resources and information? Others might be intimidated to do so or feel like others should work as hard as they do to gain success. Why do you feel differently?

I texted back:

> It is more blessed to give than to receive. And do not forget to do good and to share with others, for with such sacrifices, God is pleased.
> Hebrews 13:16

I want to share my heart with you. I took the time out of many busy days, meeting with my team at 7 PM, sometimes right after picking up dinner for my family, and sometimes having the meeting while I was driving, to share with you as much information as I could, making it as relatable and applicable as I could, to help change your life.

Although I recently received some awards that are milestone moments that I'll always be proud of, my ultimate goal is to do what pleases God. To do good and share with others pleases Him. The awards are very much appreciated, and getting publicly recognized for my civic and community efforts is nice but knowing that some people took my advice and broke the generational financial curse for their families is what fuels me and fills me with joy.

Giving back this way is the best investment I can make with God and my fellow man. I have found this to be the best, most unshakeable strategy there is. There is no market, cryptocurrency, or monetary value that blesses like the constant source that's been here since before the beginning of time and will carry on until infinity.

Like most things, helping people also comes with its set of challenges. Some people are only out for themselves and misuse my time, trust, and value. However, those of us whose purpose is to honor God in this way find the energy and wherewithal to keep helping and growing despite those with selfish intentions.

WHY?

In the bustling heart of Metropolis City, a young woman named Norma stood at a crossroads in her life. Fresh out of university, she had dreams as vast as the sky but was plagued by the fears and uncertainties that often accompany new beginnings. Her goal was clear: to build a successful career in sustainable architecture, creating buildings that harmonize with nature and help heal the planet.

One evening, as Norma walked through an old neighborhood, she stumbled upon an abandoned building. Its grandeur, though faded, spoke of a time when it was the jewel of the community. Intrigued, she ventured inside. Dust particles danced in the sunlight streaming through broken windows, and the air was thick with history and untold stories.

In the midst of the decaying grandeur, Norma found an old leather-bound journal. It belonged to an architect named Alexander, who had designed the building over a century ago. Alexander's entries revealed his passion for architecture, his struggles against societal norms, and his relentless pursuit of innovation. He wrote of nights spent pouring over blueprints by candlelight, of failures that nearly broke him, and of the small victories that fueled his spirit.

One entry struck a chord with Norma. Alexander wrote, "The path to success is not a straight road but a winding journey through valleys of self-doubt and mountains of perseverance. Every brick laid, every challenge faced, and every tear shed is a testament to our commitment to our dreams. The true measure of success is not in the accolades or wealth but in the impact we leave behind and the legacy we build."

Norma closed the journal, her heart pounding with newfound determination. Alexander's words resonated deeply. She realized that her journey to success wasn't just about achieving her goals but about the growth and transformation she would undergo along the way. It was about the buildings she would design that could change lives, the sustainable practices she would pioneer, and the inspiration she could provide to future generations.

With renewed purpose, Norma decided to restore the old building, transforming it into a community center that would serve as a beacon of sustainability and innovation. The restoration project became her first major undertaking, symbolizing the start of her personal journey to success.

Through sleepless nights, moments of doubt, and relentless hard work, Norma persevered. The community rallied behind her, and together, they breathed new life into the building. When the project was completed, it stood as a testament to the power of dreams and the impact of one person's dedication.

Norma's journey was far from over, but she had taken the first step. She understood that success was not just a destination but a continuous journey of learning, growing, and making a difference. And as she looked at the revitalized building, she knew that her personal journey to success was not just for herself but for the world she aimed to improve.

So, why should one embark on their personal journey to success? Because within that journey lies the power to transform dreams into reality, to overcome obstacles with resilience, and to leave a lasting impact that inspires others to chase their own dreams. Success is not merely about reaching the top but about the legacy we create and the lives we touch along the way.

Sure, there will be suffering—regardless of who you are. You can be born to a billionaire or to poverty in a home flooded with cockroaches when the lights go out, but it's not meant to beat you; it's meant to strengthen you. Everything worth achieving will require sacrifice, going through adversity, and continual growth despite the trials and tribulations.

This isn't just for Americans; it's for anyone on one of the seven continents. Sure, there is an uphill battle at times, but that battle is not insurmountable. You must have a realistic view of the world and know it's par for the course to sacrifice short-term for long-term gains.

Resiliency cannot be overstated. Mike Tyson once said: "Everyone has a plan 'till they get punched in the mouth." Understand that the plan you started will most likely not be the plan that gets you through. You have to be resilient sometimes, but wise enough to know when to pivot. For those who share my faith, allow your resiliency to rest on the knowledge that God would not let you get this far only to leave you stranded.

What will ultimately define you is not how many times you've fallen but rather how many times you've gotten back up. Take comfort in knowing that you only have to get up one more time than you've fallen. You can't lose if you never quit.

Realize that you were created with a unique purpose, and then go on a self-discovery journey to identify it. The Creator has a purpose for your life, and following it is greater than any issues you could encounter. He birthed you with your purpose inside of you. Once you realize and discover it, setting and walking the path to obtaining it becomes much more manageable.

NEVER SETTLE

Never settle. Never get comfortable in terms of goal setting and obtaining. I recently had lunch with a friend who has been promoted over and over and is now in the C-suite of one of the largest financial services institutions in the state of Florida. She doesn't have a boss, per se, even though she still works for a company. She doesn't need more money or another fancy title at this point in her career. She told me that one side of her pulls her to stay where she is and retire comfortably. Yet, the other side of her pulls her to complete her training as a CEO and launch into leading a company or starting her own. Which side do you think is going to win?

She said, "This isn't just about my career; it's about legacy. I aspire to get the highest level I can and bring others up with me."

Having a growth mindset means never getting comfortable and knowing it's never just about you. It's about who you can bring with you, who you can inspire, who you can lead, what you can teach, what you can sow, and where you should sow it.

The world will try everything it can to strip you of your confidence. Being confident of who you are and who you are meant to be is essential to success and happiness. Be confident and know you have or can get access to what you need to reach your goal. Use the power of your words and give yourself doses of Positive Self-Talk. Speak your reality into existence. Say to the mountain confidently—"Move."

Don't underestimate the power of consistency. Success is a product of consistent, good habits. It's not so much about your wisdom, knowledge, a theory you picked up from a book, or a nugget you picked up on social media that will bring you to the gates of success—it's all combined, applied consistently enough that it becomes a habit. Successful habits create successful people.

TIME MANAGEMENT

If I were to pass today, some would mourn, but after time, I would be forgotten, and time would continue to run. Others will pass on, and the cycle will continue. I've learned that you can't manage time. There's a beginning point of time for you and an endpoint. Between those two is the only time you have to live an extraordinary life and create a legacy. You can't manage time, but you can manage what YOU do, say, or don't do in the time you have.

Twenty-two years ago, I was creating a business plan with my sister to start a business. She passed away the night that we closed on the business. I was thrown into the deep, alone. I didn't have the power to manage time and tell it to stop so that I could have the proper time to grieve. It kept going. Whether I was in tears or suffering through a severe bout with depression, I had to manage myself wisely and make our (my sister and mine) dream come to life.

PROCRASTINATION

Avoid distractions as often as possible. I'm not suggesting you work 16-hour days and never let off the gas. It's one thing to take a week off to get energized and another to take a month to binge-watch shows.

This book embodies my experiences and ways to achieve success, but it's also the product of Time Management, Habits, and Prioritization.

EMOTIONAL INTELLIGENCE

Emotional Intelligence is the greatest competency and skill set everyone needs, whether in a leadership position, a husband, wife, child, student, teacher, pastor, or anyone else. If you can manage your emotions, you can best handle any great or catastrophic event that befalls you. If you're the type that flies off the handle, that goes from 0 to 10 in a flash, you will not be trusted or given real authority.

The best way to teach kids emotional intelligence is by being firm and forcing them to stay on track. If your college-student child wants $500 to spend on a road trip with his friends, deny it and remind him that it's time to focus and study for the big exam coming up. Even if they throw a tantrum, stand your ground. They need to know the world won't give them anything, no matter how much they pout. If they learn how to harness emotional intelligence, they'll leave the house to make their lives with the best skillset required.

WHERE'S YOUR HEART?

Money. Matthew 6:21: "Wherever your treasure is, there your heart will also be."

As a businessman, it's common for me to check the accounts often—many times, more than once daily. However, I'm mindful of my relationship with money and that it does not come before my relationship with God. This is why, every morning, I read scripture and meditate/pray before I ever check my bank accounts.

In doing that, I show my heart is with God first, and that's what I treasure. I do everything I know to be a good steward of my professional and personal finances, but that doesn't come before God. Having that type of relationship with God and money puts things into perspective.

Money is a tool, nothing more and nothing less. It's not good, nor is it evil. It's totally neutral. We make it good or bad depending on what we use it on. It's a powerful tool, to be sure. Money has the ability to get you to whatever station in life you want to be, but you must manage it and not be led by it. If you misuse this tool or ignorantly throw it away, you'll find yourself in a bad situation and needing help from others who use it better. Money is what you make it. The best thing to do with money is to use it to make more and bless others.

This is the road map to follow to reach your destination of success. It consists of real, practical, doable things that don't require a specific skill set or a degree. Implement the teachings consistently, and who knows, you may one day write your own book on how others can succeed.

CHAPTER 19
MAGNUM OPUS

YOUR GREAT WORK

As we conclude, I want you to understand that you are writing your Magnum Opus = Great Work. You have read this entire book because you are the Chosen One in your family to do Great Work. Please do not misunderstand; there can be more than "One" in a family. It could be to continue a prosperous legacy set by your parents or forefathers, or it could be that you are the one to break the financial generational curse your family has suffered through. Either way, you are Chosen to become successful.

I urge you to stay focused on your destiny. There will always be setbacks—trials and tribulations, situations, or people that knock you off your path. Life will keep setting up roadblocks and barriers, no matter who you are. However, if your prevailing thoughts continue to be on your goals and if your actions bring you closer to them daily, you will find the success that, perhaps, has eluded your family. If you let yourself get distracted, you will lose the battle.

The 22-plus years of entrepreneurship continue to accumulate. As it does, my Magnum Opus continues to expand. I may not be the one to write my final work, and that's all right. Maybe my children, a mentee, or some other concerned individual will etch my Great Work into the annals of history.

My immediate concern is this: your breakthrough today, is other people's breakthrough tomorrow. Just know that you will suffer the most, as a chosen one. Your breakthrough in life is not just for you...it is for other people too. It is for your kin.

Despite potential persecution and hardships, remain undeterred. Your sacrifices will not be in vain, as future generations will look back with gratitude for the impact you've made. Your name and platform will become instrumental tools for others to achieve success.

Being a Chosen One is akin to a dairy cow producing milk—it comprehends that its purpose is to provide for others. The cow does not drink its own milk. Similarly, the gifts bestowed upon you by a higher power are meant to be shared, impacting the lives of those around you in a positive and transformative manner.

For the last 17 years, I have not depended on a job, a salary, or a company to provide for my family and me. It's all been on me—just the way I prefer it. As John Locke so eloquently put it, "the true meaning of freedom is owning the value of your own labor." You can have a great life through education and a great position. However, for most people, I believe entrepreneurship is the gateway to financial freedom.

Through this book, I've asked you to conduct a deep, honest inner search and find your unique purpose. Your Journey to Success is tied to it. I never lost sight of mine, even when I had already obtained my master's degree and showed up to day labor. Find yourself, and you'll start on your Magnum Opus.

BECOME THE BEST VERSION OF YOU

As we come to a close, I'd like you to envision yourself twelve months from now. Envision how your life will look after you have applied the principles of success I have outlined for you. Crystalize the image of your life after living for a year, firing on all cylinders, and daily showing up for yourself and your loved ones. If you can hold this vision in your head, you can one day live it in real life.

Where would you live? How would your relationship be with your spouse or significant other? How would you relate to your siblings and children? Would they look up to you more? Would your voice hold more attention? What car would you drive? Does the best version of you look like a healthier you? What size pants or dress do you wear? What topics of conversation would you have with others—are they about business, serving the community, or mentoring others?

If you follow my Journey to Success, you may not have it all in just one year, but you'll have some of it, and then you'll notice something you didn't expect—your vision for yourself will get bigger, brighter, happier, and stronger.

No one can stop you except you. Get out of your own way. Be your biggest cheerleader. Work on yourself more than anything else. If you need help, I'm here for you.

Stay connected with me at www.garyhartfield.com.

Follow me on social media at @garyhartfield.

If you have a group you believe would benefit from my advice, don't hesitate to get in touch with me. I'd be honored to speak about life, prosperity, and resilience with them. I can be reached at: info@garyhartfield.com.

Lastly, I'll leave you with this: trust the Law of Accumulation. The more you do, the more confidence you get, the more momentum you pick up—the better life you'll live and the better legacy you'll leave. Be bold enough to destroy the areas of lack that have hindered you, but be smart enough to get the proper tutelage along the way. You are an inheritor of two beautiful worlds—the one in heaven and the one on earth. Live up to your calling and impact your world.

CHAPTER 20
STRAIGHT FROM THE HEART

One of my most profound life lessons occurred in 2023. My nephew, Noah Goodson, had been diagnosed with Osteosarcoma, a rare form of cancer a year or so earlier. As he valiantly endured treatment, he lived each day with a smile and unending courage. Noah had no fear of dying. His focus was on living.

During the last series of treatments at Moffitt Cancer Center in Tampa, FL., he stayed with me at my home. I had the opportunity to watch him, talk to him, spend time with him, and ultimately learn a profound lesson from him. Although he looked up to me, as Uncle G, to give him strength and guidance, the opposite was true. He encouraged me and gave me a new outlook on life and on living life on purpose.

During one of our conversations in the evening, after his treatment, we were talking about how he felt and what the doctors had to say about his progress. At that time, Noah shared with me that the doctors advised him that he no longer needed to come for treatment. He had been given a prognosis that he had six months to live. I stood at the door to his bedroom, and I couldn't breathe. My heart was broken. My soul was disturbed…I wanted to cry. I wanted to console him but didn't know how. Surprisingly, Noah was not shaken by this news. He was still his usual jovial self.

During this time with Noah, I realized our time together was not a coincidence. Noah's life experience was intimately shared to help guide me on my way.

As I made my way from Noah's room back to my home office, I noticed that the air in my room was thick and heavy with my confusion, sadness, and grief. I sat at my desk, staring at the words scrawled on a small piece of paper taped to my computer monitor: "Do Hard Better." It has become my daily mantra, a reminder of Noah's strength. This mantra became my commitment to growth, resilience, and the pursuit of success.

In a world that often seeks shortcuts and the path of least resistance, "Do Hard Better" stood out as a beacon of defiance. It wasn't about choosing the easiest route but about embracing challenges, pushing boundaries, and thriving in the face of adversity. Life, as I had come to understand, was a series of hurdles, and the mantra served as a constant reminder that the secret to a meaningful existence lay in doing hard things exceptionally well.

The concept wasn't about glorifying struggle for the sake of it; rather, it was a call to action for those who aspired to make a difference. It was a philosophy that encouraged individuals to shatter the limitations of comfort and complacency to cultivate a mindset that reveled in the discomfort of growth. I have learned that life never gets easier; instead, I must get better at navigating its complexities.

As I looked at the words on my monitor, I felt a surge of determination. Life's challenges were inevitable, but so was my commitment to doing hard things better. The mantra had become more than just words; it was a philosophy that redefined my approach to life. With a renewed sense of purpose, I learned to lean into the challenges ahead, ready to embrace the difficulties and emerge on the other side, having done hard better.

Then, a thought came to me that I couldn't shake. What if the angel of life appeared to me and said, "Gary, your time is up. It is time for you to die."

Would my response be, "I need another week, another year…. can you please give me another fifty-three years to fulfill my purpose?"

I envisioned the angel of life's stern being, "Gary, what have you done with the time you've been gifted? Whose fault is it that you misused it? What could convince The Creator that you would suddenly do anything with a little more time?"

To this end, my dear reader, I ask, "What have you done with the time you have been given? More importantly, what will you do with the time you still have?"

I owe my best efforts to my parents, my family, my community, my legacy, my future, and my creator. To what and to whom do you owe your best efforts? I urge you, from the depths of my being, *Do Hard Better*, and maximize the only life you've been gifted.

My nephew, Noah Goodson, passed away from complications due to cancer on July 18, 2023. He was 28 years old.

Uncle G loves you, Noah; thanks for the lessons.

ABOUT THE AUTHOR

Gary T. Hartfield has committed his life's work to empowerment and advocation based on his personal belief that "God gave him a resonant heart that beats for justice for everyone but especially for those who are oppressed and intentionally held back". He has used this gift as a platform in his professional endeavors as the CEO of many Residential Group Homes throughout the state of Florida that serve the elderly and developmentally disabled and as owner and CEO of Serenity Village Insurance & Consulting, a full-service property and casualty agency delivering solutions to mitigate risk for business owners.

Born and raised in DeFuniak Springs, FL, Gary dreamed of wanting to be the change agent that would ensure his family and community's success. This passion is what fueled his success in the academic arena allowing him to obtain his Bachelor's of Science in Electronic Engineering Technology from Florida Agricultural & Mechanical University (FAMU), Master's in Business Administration from the University of West Florida and an Executive Leadership Certification from Cornell University.

Gary's love of education is not only demonstrated in his personal pursuit but also in his desire to uplift others with knowledge and information because of his great desire to embody the change he wishes to see in the world. Gary is a "social engineer" who has found innovative ways to impact the business and non-profit communities. His innovation and contributions have been celebrated locally and nationally. However, of all his greatest achievements, Gary considers his most significant accomplish-ment to be his role as a present and supportive father. He strives daily to be engaged as a provider and protector for each of his children.

It is Gary's desire that the lessons he has obtained on his road to success found in this book may ignite a flame within the reader to encourage them on their path to greatness and excellence.

Stay connected with me at www.garyhartfield.com.

Follow me on social media @GaryHartfield.

I can be reached at: info@garyhartfield.com.

ACKNOWLEDGMENTS

Writing "The Journey to Success" has been a profound experience, and it would not have been possible without the support, guidance, and encouragement of many individuals.

First and foremost, I want to express my deepest gratitude to my family. To my mother and father, Norma and Booketee Hartfield, whose unwavering support and belief in me have been a constant source of strength. Your love and encouragement have been the bedrock upon which my journey has been built. Rest in Peace.

I am immensely grateful to my friends and colleagues who provided invaluable insights, feedback, and encouragement throughout the writing process. Your constructive criticism and words of motivation have been instrumental in shaping this book.

A heartfelt thank you goes out to my mentor, whose wisdom and guidance have been pivotal in my personal and professional growth. Your belief in my potential and your willingness to share your knowledge have been truly inspiring.

To my brand director and publishing team, thank you for your dedication and meticulous attention to detail. Your expertise and passion for this project have been crucial in bringing this book to life.

I would also like to acknowledge the many individuals who shared their stories and experiences with me. Your openness and honesty have enriched this book in ways I could never have imagined.

Lastly, to my readers, thank you for embarking on this journey with me. I hope "The Journey to Success" resonates with you and provides inspiration and guidance on your own path to success.

With gratitude,

Gary T. Hartfield

RECOMMENDED READING

1. Lead or Get out the Way, Gary Vein
2. Your Next Five Moves, Patrick Bet-David
3. How to Win Friends & Influence People, Dale Carneigie
4. High Performance Habits, Brendon Burchard
5. Leadershift, John C. Maxwell
6. The Diary of a CEO, Steven Bartlett
7. Bowling Alone: Revised and Updated, Robert D. Putnam
8. Emotional Intelligence 2.0, Jean Greaves and Travis Bradberry
9. The Law of Success, Napoleon Hill
10. Disruptive Thinking, T.D. Jakes
11. The Color of Law, Richard Rothstein
12. Crushing, T.D. Jakes
13. The 4 Disciplines of Execution: Revised and Update, Sean Covey, Scott Thele
14. The E-Myth Revisited, Michael E. Gerber
15. Atomic Habits, James Clear
16. Think and Grow Rich: A Black Choice, Napoleon Hill and Dennis Kimbro
17. Think and Grow Rich, Napoleon Hill
18. The Wisdom of Sundays, Oprah Winfrey

19. Smart Brevity, Jim VandeHei, Mike Allen
20. Long Obedience in the Same Direction, Eugen H. Peterson

www.ingramcontent.com/pod-product-compliance
Lightning Source LLC
Chambersburg PA
CBHW060524130626
46553CB00002B/644
* 9 7 9 8 9 9 1 2 1 9 7 0 9 *